ROYAL TROON
GOLF CLUB

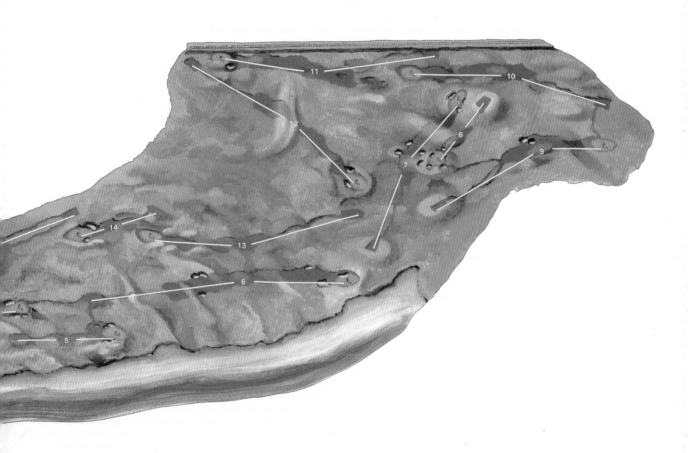

THE OPEN CHAMPIONSHIP 1997

OFFICIAL ANNUAL IN ASSOCIATION WITH

THE OPEN CHAMPIONSHIP 1997

OFFICIAL ANNUAL IN ASSOCIATION WITH

WRITERS

ROBERT SOMMERS
MICHAEL MCDONNELL
ROBERT GREEN
ANDREW FARRELL
ALISTER NICOL
JOHN HOPKINS

PHOTOGRAPHERS

MICHAEL COHEN
FRED VUICH

EDITOR

BEV NORWOOD

AUTHORISED BY THE
CHAMPIONSHIP COMMITTEE
OF THE ROYAL AND ANCIENT
GOLF CLUB OF ST ANDREWS

THE CONTRIBUTORS DEDICATE THIS BOOK TO THE MEMORY OF
GEORGE WILSON AND MICHAEL WILLIAMS,
BOTH OF WHOM SUPPORTED THE PREVIOUS 13 EDITIONS.

HAZLETON PUBLISHING LTD
3 Richmond Hill, Richmond, Surrey TW10 6RE

Published 1997 by Hazleton Publishing Ltd
Copyright © 1997 The Championship Committee Merchandising
Limited

Statistics of 126th Open Championship produced on a
Unisys Computer System

Fred Vuich is staff photographer for GOLF Magazine (USA)
and photographs are courtesy of Times Mirror Magazines, Inc.

Photograph on page 60 courtesy of Allsport Photographic Plc.

A CIP catalogue record for this book is available
from the British Library

ISBN: 1-874557-77-2

Typeset by Davis Design
Printed in Great Britain
by Butler & Tanner, Frome, Somerset

CONTENTS

INTRODUCTION

BY SIR RICHARD EVANS CBE
Chief Executive
British Aerospace plc

The breathtaking view across the Firth of Clyde from Royal Troon provided the perfect backdrop to the 1997 Open Golf Championship which, for the second year running, was played in perfect British summer weather.

The calm conditions meant that perhaps Troon did not present its fiercest challenge to the players. By the fourth day, many of the world's finest golfers had fallen by the wayside and, as is so often the case, the eventual winner was not ranked among the favourites.

One of the main features of this year's Open Championship was the accent on youth generated by the decision to admit under-18s free of charge for the first time. Everyone was anxious to see the young American sensation Tiger Woods live in action in the UK since his historic win at Augusta and this created an electric atmosphere amongst the crowds. In the end, of course, it was another young American, Justin Leonard, who stormed home over the closing holes to become the Open Champion and to give inspiration to the next generation of golfers.

I would like to thank the Royal and Ancient Golf Club and the Championship Committee at Royal Troon for staging such a memorable event. British Aerospace was again proud to be part of it and we look forward to 1998 when the Open returns to Lancashire and Royal Birkdale.

Sir Richard Evans CBE

THE CHAMPIONSHIP COMMITTEE

CHAIRMAN

P. W. J. GREENHOUGH

DEPUTY CHAIRMAN

G. B. HOBART

COMMITTEE

P. E. BECHMANN
A. BRODIE
R. M. BURNS
J. J. N. CAPLAN
A. J. HILL
G. HUDDY
A. J. N. LOUDON
M. S. R. LUNT
J. L. S. PASQUILL
N. M. STEPHENS

BUSINESS SUB-COMMITTEE CHAIRMAN

R. D. JAMES

RULES SUB-COMMITTEE CHAIRMAN

T. B. TAYLOR

ADDITIONAL MEMBER

M. N. DOYLE
COUNCIL OF NATIONAL GOLF UNIONS

SECRETARY

M. F. BONALLACK, OBE

CHAMPIONSHIP SECRETARY

D. HILL

ASSISTANT SECRETARY (CHAMPIONSHIPS)

D. R. WEIR

ASSISTANT SECRETARY (CHAMPIONSHIPS)

A. E. FARQUHAR

INTRODUCTION

BY P. W. J. GREENHOUGH
Chairman of Championship Committee
Royal and Ancient Golf Club of St Andrews

For the third consecutive year an American won the Open Championship. This time Justin Leonard, a former US Amateur champion, shattered the field with a fourth round of 65 to win by three shots from Darren Clarke and Jesper Parnevik.

Billy McLachlan and his team of green-keepers ensured that the Royal Troon links were in magnificent condition and, apart from the first day when the wind blew, the players were tested to the limit by the natural challenges of the course.

The largest ever crowd at an Open at Royal Troon were looking forward to watching Tiger Woods. They were not disappointed, particularly with his third round of 64, but he was unable to repeat such scoring in his other rounds and finished in a tie for 24th place.

Over 2,200 competitors entered the Championship, and the Royal and Ancient Championship Committee are very grateful to the 14 Regional and four Final Qualifying Clubs that helped us to reduce the original entry to the 156 players that contested the Championship.

The Captain, Committee and Members of Royal Troon were most enthusiastic and helpful, both during and before the Championship. Their support was very much appreciated by the Championship Committee.

Finally, we are grateful to British Aerospace for their continued support for this official Annual, and we should like to thank the photographers and writers whose contributions have helped to record a memorable Championship in the following pages.

P. W. J. Greenhough

Peter Greenhough.

FOREWORD

BY JUSTIN LEONARD

It seemed as though standing on the 18th green at Royal Troon, in the late afternoon shadows and sunlight holding the Silver Claret Jug, everything had come together. It was an incredible moment that I shall never forget. I will always remember the emotion I experienced when my thoughts turned to my family, friends, teacher, golf competitors, and history. All the experiences that I had gained from each of those seemed to meet in that place at that time on the 18th green. Maybe they were bottled up in that silver jug, and as I was fortunate to get my hands on it and realising it was mine, I was rewarded with a feeling of being at the centre of all those things that I had wanted, worked for, and dreamed.

Careful examination of the engravings on the Claret Jug of the former winners caused me to wonder if they had similar feelings. I know they felt extreme emotions, whether they showed them or not, and they were proud of their accomplishments. Each of my family and friends that have held it feel some of those same feelings of pride that I have, and their contribution to whatever I am as a golfer, son, brother, family member, or friend comes to their mind. To me, the Claret Jug is not a "jug" at all, it's not a trophy, it's not a place to record history. It is a symbol of good things that have come together for the 125 others that have held it at that magical moment in time, and it is a challenge to perhaps another 126 to attain it, hold it, and experience it.

Justin Leonard

The Postage Stamp, at 126 yards the shortest hole in Open Championship golf, has witnessed scores from Gene Sarazen's

hole-in-one to Herman Tissies' 15 strokes.

ROUND ROYAL TROON

No. 1 364 Yards, Par 4

A gentle introduction where the drive is placed to the right side of the fairway away from the two left-hand bunkers so that the prospects of an opening birdie are good, provided the four greenside traps are avoided.

No. 2 391 Yards, Par 4

Three cross bunkers are within range downwind from the tee, and the wise choice is to play short for a more comfortable approach to a pear-shaped green protected by more bunkers.

No. 3 379 Yards, Par 4

A narrow fairway is crossed by a burn which could be within range downwind. So the correct ploy is to come up short of the danger for an unhindered approach to the kidney-shaped green which has two bunkers to the left and another on the right.

No. 4 557 Yards, Par 5

In the 1989 championship, this was ranked as the second easiest hole on the course with 16 eagles recorded. The paradox is that it offers more likely reward of a birdie or better if played cautiously so that the trouble en route between tee and green is eliminated.

No. 5 210 Yards, Par 3

A long and intimidating one-shotter that demands more club than it seems, because there are no prizes for just scraping on to the front edge. The tee shot must find the heart of the green so that the deep bunkers either side are taken out of play.

No. 6 577 Yards, Par 5

The longest hole on the Open Championship rota and the grim area where Bobby Clampett came to grief in the 1982 championship and never truly recovered from a triple-bogey 8. Can be reached safely in three strokes by playing short of the left-hand greenside bunkers, but the big hitters get home in two.

No. 7 402 Yards, Par 4

From an elevated tee, the drive must avoid bunkers on both sides of the fairway set in the corner of this left-to-right dogleg to allow a simple approach to a well-guarded green which slopes sharply upward from front to back.

No. 8 126 Yards, Par 3

The shortest hole in Open Championship golf and beset by cavernous bunkers on all sides. The only safe mistake is to overhit the green from the tee for a reasonable chip shot back. Timidity and indecision are heavily punished, sometimes beyond repair.

No. 9 423 Yards, Par 4

The most difficult hole on the outward nine in the 1989 championship, it must be treated with respect and requires a tee shot short of the left-hand bunkers to allow sight of the two-tiered green through a narrow gully.

No. 10 438 Yards, Par 4

No bunkers, but still a notoriously difficult hole because of the blind tee shot with a driver, followed by a second shot to the green which falls away on both sides and offers itself as a reluctant target.

No. 11 463 Yards, Par 4

Reduced from an original par-5 and 481 yards, it has become a most formidable par-4, with gorse bushes flanking the fairway which falls to the right and towards the stone wall and railway line, particularly beside the green.

No. 12 431 Yards, Par 4

The fairway curves to the right to present an undemanding tee shot, but the flagstick can be difficult to attack on this narrow two-tiered green unless the Mark Calcavecchia approach is adopted. He pitched into the hole for his birdie on his way to winning the 1989 championship.

No. 13 465 Yards, Par 4

Herewith begins the most difficult finishing stretch in Open Championship golf — certainly the longest into the prevailing wind. It requires two powerful strokes over rolling terrain to find the green. No bunkers needed to sharpen this test.

No. 14 179 Yards, Par 3

Deceptively simple hole which looks straightforward enough but is protected by three bunkers. The wise move is to play long to the wide part of the green and remove the threat of the bunkers from play.

No. 15 457 Yards, Par 4

Only the longest and straightest drive will suffice on this hole and must finish between the fairway bunkers so that a second shot can be negotiated to a sunken and well-protected green. The gamblers will play the ball to the right in hopes of a lucky bounce off the bank.

No. 16 542 Yards, Par 5

Another critical choice for the very long hitters on whether to carry the ditch which crosses the fairway to allow a short, more direct route to the green. Failure brings its own penalties, and for those who take three strokes to get home, the second must be played left to open up the long, narrow green.

No. 17 223 Yards, Par 3

The most difficult hole in the 1989 championship. Anything is possible from the tee depending on the weather — from driver to long iron — but it is imperative to stay on the green, which tends to discard the tee shot into deep bunkers on either side.

No. 18 452 Yards, Par 4

Not a gentle conclusion, because the carry to the fairway is 225 yards and becomes more difficult as the championship concludes. The green is vulnerable to even a long iron, but its defences include an array of bunkers as well as an out-of-bounds path just in front of the clubhouse.

A TEST OF SKILL AND STRENGTH

BY MICHAEL McDONNELL

The true function of a championship links is not simply to serve as the playing field upon which superior skills can be demonstrated, but rather to take on the role of menacing adversary to an aspiring champion until he has proved beyond doubt he is the rightful choice.

It is therefore an active confrontation in which the ambitious candidate must remain focused on a dangerous opponent who, through the vagaries of wind and tide, quite apart from punishing terrain and architectural design, can present a new and quite overwhelming task with almost every stroke that is played.

The eternal strength of links golf has always been that it tests the man as much as his golf. Indeed the club motto at Royal Troon "Tam Arte Quam Marte" gives full and fair warning of the necessary requirements for a successful foray over its fairways along the shores of the Firth of Clyde on the west coast of Scotland.

The translation is "As much

Royal Troon has hosted seven Opens.

by skill as by strength" and has been the key to all previous triumphs at this club founded in 1878, and in fact represents the core of a game plan that was in existence long before modern terminology defined it as such. Without question, it was the basis for Arnold Palmer's success in 1962 when he won his second successive Open title.

That year Troon's fairways were hard and fiery and presented a daunting prospect, particularly to American challengers who had left the lush and watered confines of their own tour to take on this alien style of golf in its most basic form.

It was a task that proved to be beyond the burgeoning ability of a 22-year-old newcomer who had caused a sensation only a few weeks earlier by snatching the US Open title from Palmer in a play-off. By his own admission, Jack Nicklaus was not yet ready for this kind of golf and finished 29 strokes behind the winner in his first Open.

There were, however, extenuating circumstances for his failure to adjust quickly enough. He was uncomfortable with the smaller British golf ball then in use, and his new clubs were not right for him either. Then, too, he was dismayed to find he had been given the last starting time on the first day at 3.45 pm — with a marker. Only when Irish international Joe Carr reminded officials that this was hardly the proper treatment for the US Open champion was he moved into a threesome — but still put off last.

Even so, Big Jack's problems were purely personal and of little interest to the Scottish fans who had come to see Arnie, the main attraction, tackle Troon in his own swashbuckling style. His transformation of golf had begun only two years earlier when he burst upon the scene at St Andrews and narrowly missed the title by a stroke.

The greater achievement at St Andrews had been to brush away the cobwebs from a game that, for the most part, had been the domain of the rich and middle-aged. Arnie suddenly brought excitement and drama to the sport, and it was said that he clambered to the first tee like a boxer climbing into the ring and looking for a fight. He played fearlessly and fero-

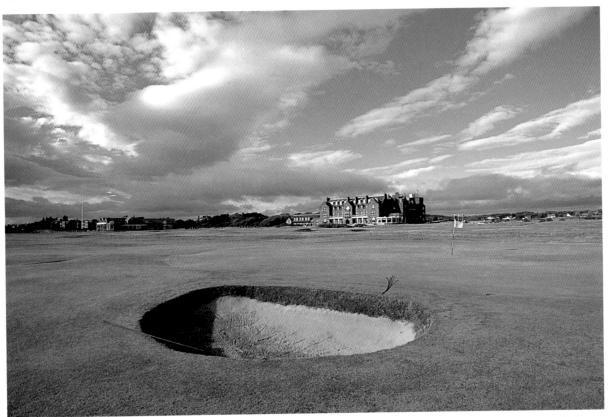

The prospects are good for a birdie on the 364-yard first hole, provided the four greenside bunkers are avoided.

ciously and never backed off no matter what the risk. In short, he played the game the way everybody else in the world wanted to play it.

It is estimated that between 20,000 and 30,000 turned out to see him play, and presented authorities with the first experience of modern crowd trouble in a game that hitherto had been mannerly and orderly. This was not booze-driven loutish behaviour, but simply unrestrained exuberance and delight at this new hero.

Nor did he disappoint them, though he played Troon with extreme respect, and as soon as he saw the 11th hole, then 485 yards, knew it would be the key to the round, and that whatever gains had been made on the outward run had to be protected over this stretch so as not to squander any advantage on the way home.

The tee stood on a windswept knoll, and the tee shot had to carry 230 yards of wilderness to a fairway that was only 30 yards wide and flanked to the left by gorge bushes and sloping towards a stone wall and out of bounds on the right. Despite its length, Arnie resolved to take a one iron from the tee every day, then thread a two iron between the bunkers to the small green.

In the four rounds of the tournament he had two birdies and an eagle at this hole and he also birdied it during both qualifying rounds. It was a staggering display of power, restraint and accuracy, and he went on to win with a 276 total and a six-stroke margin.

In truth, Troon had been something of a culture shock for the flamboyant Walter Hagen when he competed in the first Open there in 1923. He was the defending champion and enjoyed the millionaire lifestyle, so naturally he took over a suite in the nearby Marine Hotel beside the 18th fairway. He was dismayed to learn that professionals were not allowed to enter the clubhouse.

The Haig shrugged off such treatment and used his suite in which to change his shoes. Moreover, he went on to make a creditable defence of his title, but narrowly missed a birdie on the last hole to force a tie with the eventual winner Arthur Havers, a 26-year-old Englishman. Both were invited into the clubhouse for the presentation, but Walter declined and retired to a local pub with many of his fans.

That Open was notable for another incident when Royal and Ancient officials decreed that ribbed and punched iron clubfaces did not conform to the rules

Although one of Troon's easiest holes, the fourth should be played cautiously for the best result.

and had to be smoothed out. The decision caused considerable panic among the stars, but prompted a lot of welcome revenue in local workshops, as craftsmen got to work with their files to ensure the clubs were ready for the start of the championship.

When future historians study the revival in European golf in the second half of the 20th century, they will conclude that the switch to the 1.68-inch diameter American-size golf ball was a key factor, because of the high degree of control and shot-making required. Tom Weiskopf, the 1973 champion, earns his particular place in history as being the last man to win the Open Championship with the traditional smaller 1.62-inch diameter British golf ball.

It was a remarkable piece of adjustment by this naturally gifted athlete, who had not only lived within the giant shadow of his famous Ohio neighbour, Jack Nicklaus, but had seen so many chances slip away — sometimes through his own exasperation. However, he came to Troon with a new sense of purpose, and engaged in a dramatic duel with Johnny Miller, who weeks earlier had won the US Open.

Weiskopf was to show remarkable restraint, especially over the closing holes, when he forsook his driver in favour of a one iron, which he used at the

The seventh green is well-guarded.

The 10th is difficult because of a blind tee shot.

The 431-yard 12th features an undemanding tee shot but a narrow two-tiered green.

16th and 18th holes, just to keep the ball in play. It was a judicious strategy that some years later Greg Norman might wisely have employed on that same 18th hole. Instead he drove into sand and succumbed to Mark Calcavecchia — along with Wayne Grady — in the first aggregate four-hole Open play-off.

Before the final show-down between Weiskopf and Miller, there had been a magical moment at the Postage Stamp, the 126-yard eighth hole which is the shortest in Open Championship golf. The venerable Gene Sarazan, making a sentimental return visit, holed in one with a five iron and the next day sank his bunker shot for a birdie 2. Sadly, Sarazan missed the halfway cut, but had left his mark on Royal Troon, as it had then become, and donated the famous five iron to the authorities as a memento.

His display contrasted sharply with the nightmare of German amateur Herman Tissies in the 1950 Open won by South African Bobby Locke. That week, on a fast-running course, Locke had relied heavily on his superlative short game to prove his superiority and take his second title. Tissies is still remembered for his display at Troon, too, because he took 15 strokes at the Postage Stamp, and most of them in bunkers.

It is the nature of every sporting occasion that one man's success is invariably at the cost of another's failure. In the 1982 championship there were two obvious victims, and one of these suffered unquestionably from self-inflicted wounds that those present that day will never forget.

Bobby Clampett, a genial, curly-haired Californian, burst upon the scene with an easy grace and charm that made the game look so simple, even though he followed strict methodology. It was a doctrine that clearly paid off, because he opened with a 67 and followed it with a 66 to stand five strokes clear of Nick Price at 11-under-par 133 at the halfway stage.

These years since, Clampett may often have wondered what went wrong and why the march to glory turned into a sickening lurch into failure. Was he too complacent? Did it all seem too easy? Why did a simple drama become a ruinous crisis? For certain, Royal Troon put him to a test he could not handle and his moment was gone.

At one stage he had been seven strokes clear in the third round, but on the long sixth he hit into three bunkers for a triple-bogey 8, then dropped strokes at

The defences of the 18th hole include bunkers and an out-of-bounds path in front of the clubhouse.

another four holes to finish only one clear of the field. By the next day he had soon disappeared without trace, leaving the stage clear for Price, who was then menaced by Tom Watson.

A series of errors over the last four holes cost Price his chance, as he felt real pressure for the first time and allowed Watson to take the title and become only the fifth man in the history of the sport to win the Open championships in both the United States and Britain in the same year.

As Watson stood to acknowledge the cheering fans, he held a woollen scarf above his head bearing the words "Scotland the Brave" from a well-known national song. It was his third of an eventual four wins in that country — the fifth came in England — but the moment evoked memories of another American victory at Troon accompanied by a Scottish song. Charlie Yates, a close friend of Bobby Jones and a senior member of Augusta National, won the Amateur title in 1938, then sang "Just a wee Deoch an' Dorris" to the delighted crowd (a treat he reserved subsequently for his friends during the US Masters).

The enduring obligation Royal Troon places upon a golfer is to make the right decision at the right time or suffer the consequences. Greg Norman can bear sad testimony to this truth. He had sprinted clear in the 1989 play-off against Grady and Calcavecchia, then inexplicably decided to chip the ball from the fringe of the 17th green instead of taking a putter. The error cost him a stroke to par, and he then drove a massive distance down the last fairway into a bunker that he thought was out of reach. It cost him any hopes of the title and Calcavecchia became the champion.

Thus has Royal Troon played its major role in the historical development of the game and witnessed some of the great and inspiring moments involving the outstanding players of each generation who faced its challenge with varying degrees of fortune. There have been other unforgettable moments, too. In the final of the 1968 Amateur Championship, Michael Bonallack was in the process of handing out a fearful 7-and-6 defeat to Joe Carr when a small boy with a collecting-box approached the Irishman and asked him to contribute to a charity for the blind. Joe smiled ruefully and said, "The way I'm putting, you ought to be collecting for me!"

Happy days, but even greater memories.

Out in 32, Jim Furyk had two bogeys on the second nine, but his 67 shared the first-round lead.

ONLY FIVE ARE BELOW 70

BY ROBERT SOMMERS

In the days leading up to the 126th Open Championship, everyone, it seemed, had been struck by how well so many of the game's leading golfers had been playing. Marvels of this sort happen only rarely on the eve of one of the game's great occasions, but there it was.

At the top came defending champion Tom Lehman, who had come to Royal Troon at the peak of his game, along with Ernie Els, the US Open champion, Colin Montgomerie, Greg Norman and, of course, Tiger Woods.

Of them all, Lehman seemed the most impressive. He had come to the 71st hole of the US Open needing a birdie to force a play-off with Els but pulled his approach into a pond instead. Then the week before the Open began he had won the Gulfstream Loch Lomond World Invitational by shooting 65-66-67-67–265, five strokes ahead of Els. Ernie, meantime, had followed the US Open by winning at Westchester, New York, the next week and later placed second to Lehman at Loch Lomond.

Montgomerie had not only finished second to Els in the US Open, he had won the Compaq European Grand Prix in early June and the Murphy's Irish Open two weeks before Royal Troon.

The whole world knew about Woods. Already a phenomenal golfer at 21 years of age, he had followed what for him was a disappointing tie for 19th place in the US Open by winning the Motorola Western Open two weeks later. That was his fifth victory of the year, including the US Masters and a tournament in Thailand.

Norman had revived somewhat as well and had won the FedEx St Jude Classic, in Memphis, Tennessee, with 268, rather sensational scoring.

Indicators like this are often disappointing because golf is among the least formful of games; the best players don't necessarily win, or even threaten to win. Having a bad ball-striking day, Lehman opened with 74, Els shot 75, and Montgomerie was worst of all. Usually the straightest of drivers, Monty rarely hit a fairway and shot 76, matching the highest score he had ever shot in six previous Opens. Woods, meantime, shot a ragged 72 that could have been much better or much worse.

Of them all only Norman showed any spark, whipping around Troon in 69, two strokes under a truly mean par of 71. At the end of the day he tied for third place behind both Jim Furyk, the American with the bizarre swing, and Darren Clarke, from Portrush. Furyk and Clarke shot 67s under quite difficult conditions over a brutish golf course. With his 69, Norman tied Fred Couples and Justin Leonard, a 25-year-old Texan who had won the Kemper Open the week before the US Open.

Any score under par represented superb golf on a chilly, dreary, windy day like this. Thick grey clouds blocked out the sun through most of the day, and the wind blew in from the northwest at strengths from 20 to 30 miles an hour, turning Royal Troon into as difficult as examination of shotmaking as anyone could remember. From a field of 156 of the world's best golfers, only five men shot in the 60s, five others shot 70, and six others matched the course par of 71.

The homeward nine, difficult under any conditions, played directly into the wind, which turned this normally hard course into a brutal test of the game. Only the best ball-striking could wring results from Troon. His round over, Norman said Troon was like two golf courses — the first nine and the second nine.

"The wind meant you couldn't use your yardages," Norman said. "You have to imagine shots — see them, feel them, and use every aspect of the game. You can hit a six iron 240 yards on the first nine and only 120 yards coming back."

Tom Watson said he normally hits his one iron 225 yards, but on the second nine this day he could

Greg Norman (69) said, "We were hitting six irons 240 yards downwind and 120 yards into the wind."

count on just 190.

Norman seemed particularly proud of the two iron he played to the 11th hole, a 463-yard par-4 that runs alongside the Glasgow to Ayr railway line and whose fairway is bordered by large and prickly gorse bushes.

Describing the shot, Norman said, "I had 207 yards to go. The ball never got more than 20 feet off the ground and finished on the green 40 feet away." Not often will a player of Norman's quality claim an iron to 40 feet his best shot of a round.

The 11th was hard, but then the 13th was hard as well. Lehman is no short hitter, but after a solid drive he played a fairway wood and still fell short. Curtis Strange, who had won two US Opens, couldn't reach the 15th, at 457 yards, with a three wood, either.

The shorter hitters, in fact, had trouble reaching fairways in the strong wind. Miguel Angel Jimenez and Greg Turner couldn't reach the 18th fairway, and David Duval, who is not short, barely made it himself. It became so frustrating some suggested the R and A might consider moving some tees forward.

Not that the first nine could be managed easily; playing downwind set up impossible shots as well. Els found a problem on the first hole, which, at 364 yards, could be driven. Ernie's tee shot drifted slightly right of the green, leaving him a little pitch to a hole set behind a deep bunker. With the wind behind him though, he couldn't stop a lofted shot; instead he played a pitch-and-run left of the bunker and felt he was lucky to stop his ball within 20 feet of the hole.

Nevertheless, the homeward nine caused most of the agony by consistently taking away strokes won on the first nine. Couples, for example, went out in 31 with the wind at his back, but struggled home in 38. Both Clarke and Furyk went out in 32 and came back in 35. Norman came back in 37 after an outward 32. Those were the good scores.

Lehman went out in 34, two strokes under par, but after turning into the wind, he missed nearly every green on the second nine and came back in 40. Even so, he did better than lots of others. Els, Jose Maria Olazabal and Costantino Rocca, who came so close to winning the 1995 Open, all went out in 35s, one under par, and came back in 40 — five over. Peter

Tom Lehman (74) shot 40 on the second nine.

Jesper Parnevik (70) birdied the last three holes to finish under par.

Darren Clarke (67) went out in 32, birdieing both par-5s.

Lonard, a husky Australian who lost four years of competition because of a malaria-like disease, went out in 32 and back in 40; Peter Hedblom, who had played so well at Royal Lytham in 1996, shot 33-43; Phil Mickelson shot 35-41; Mike Bradley, three under par after eight holes, went out in 34 and back in 43, and Klas Erickson played the first nine in even-par 36 and blundered home in 49.

Ninety-three players, 60 percent of the field, shot 40 or higher on the second nine; four men other than Clarke and Furyk shot even-par 35 — among them Leonard, Nick Faldo and Jack Nicklaus — and only Jesper Parnevik shot 34. It was indeed a hard day.

Norman, though, seemed to thrive on the conditions. He teed off at 8.15 and played through the worst of the wind. Later in the day the sun broke through the overcast, the temperature climbed, and the wind eased somewhat, but he had finished by then and could sit back and watch the others struggle.

Other than his practice round, Norman hadn't played Troon since the final round of the 1989 Open, when he tore around in 64 and climbed into a tie for first place. He opened the four-hole play-off by birdieing the first two holes and yet lost to Mark Calcavecchia by driving into a fairway bunker on the 18th. He made no such mistakes this day.

As everyone else, Norman knew that to score he

Fred Couples (69) birdied five holes on the first nine.

would have to make his birdies on the outgoing nine, where the wind helped with distance. For example, after holing from 18 feet on the third for his first birdie of the day, Norman played the fourth with a driver and a six iron that rolled off the back of the green. The hole measured 557 yards. A chip to two feet and he had birdied again.

After a bogey on the fifth, a 210-yard par-3, where his six iron missed the green, Norman came to the sixth, at 577 yards the longest hole in the Open rota. A driver put him in position to reach the green, but his three iron dived into a bunker. Still, he pitched to three feet and holed for his birdie, and added another at the seventh, where he played a low running shot up the slope to the hole, cut in the green's front-right corner just beyond a bunker. He made his final birdie of the day on the ninth, a par-4 of 423 yards, where he drove with a four iron to stay short of a pair of bunkers set in a hillside. A nine iron to six feet and he had gone out in 32.

He could make no further headway against par, and indeed had to play forthright golf to save himself from losing more than two strokes coming in. He could have done better, but he three-putted the 18th from 10 feet.

Couples, meanwhile, played half an hour behind Norman, and in his usual unconcerned manner

Angel Cabrera (70) overcame a 6 on the 13th.

A big gallery watched Tiger Woods (72) in a round that could have been much better or much worse.

Davis Love III (70) was four under after six.

looked as if he might shoot to the front. With his lazy, fluid swing — he just raises the club through its backswing, then drops his hands and whips the club through the ball — he birdied five holes on the first nine, including, of course, the two par-5s. He didn't play so well coming in and lost strokes on both the 10th and 11th, two of the three hardest par-4s, and another on the 18th.

At first the big gallery following Woods felt they might be rewarded with one of the day's best rounds, but after a fine start, which dropped him to two under par after six holes, Woods began losing strokes. Only a strong finish with two birdies on the last three holes saved him for another day.

The first hole gave a hint that this might not be Tiger's day. He began by trying to drive the first green but caught the left greenside bunker instead. From an awkward stance, with his left leg outside the bunker and his right in it, Woods bladed the ball across the green into a bunker on the other side. He still managed a par 4.

Reaching the fourth, he made the gallery gasp with a drive of 435 yards. His ball stopped rolling about seven yards short of a yellow dot painted in the fairway to mark a distance of 115 yards to the green. With a nine-iron second he missed the green but still

Phil Mickelson (76) made six bogeys on the second nine.

Colin Montgomerie (76) had seven bogeys in nine holes.

saved a birdie. His long game astounded the spectators. After another birdie at the sixth, he drove a greenside bunker on the 402-yard seventh and made only a par 4, and he bogeyed the eighth, the Postage Stamp, Troon's most famous hole. At 126 yards it is the shortest hole on the Open rota, but it can be the most devilish. Woods bunkered his tee shot and two-putted from six feet.

One under par after nine, Woods' round fell apart on the 11th, where he made 7, wiping out the good work he had done on the early holes. Still, with 72, he remained a contender.

With much of the gallery waiting to watch either Woods or Lehman, not many spectators saw the co-leaders. They played in successive groupings, Furyk at 12.15 and Clarke 10 minutes later. They were a contrasting pair, Clarke, from Northern Ireland, a little pudgy but with a conventionally powerful swing, and Furyk, originally from West Chester, Pennsylvania, a suburb of Philadelphia, tall and lithe and with championship golf's most eccentric motion.

Furyk takes the club back on a path outside the line of flight, then twirls it above his head like Tommy Dorsey signaling Bunny Berrigan to take a riff, drops his hands into proper position as he begins his downswing, and looks like everyone else at the moment of

Ernie Els (75) bogeyed three of the last four.

Kim Jong Duck (77) was once on the leaderboard.

Ian Woosnam (71) was one under on the last five.

Amateur Barclay Howard (70) shared sixth place.

contact. David Feherty, who once played in these events but now talks about them on television, said Furyk's swing reminds him of an octopus falling from a tree.

His swing is the more difficult to understand because he is the son of a golf professional. Asked about his method, Furyk admitted he had little interest in technical points and said, "I couldn't grasp angles and club positions. My father is a great teacher because he takes what the pupil has and works with that."

Furyk, aged 27, played his first Open at Royal Lytham a year earlier and opened with 68. He had had no experience playing links courses, but on the way over from the United States he convinced himself that, "Hey, it's still golf. You've still got to get the ball into the hole in as few strokes as possible."

That he did. He began with a bold drive that pulled up 20 yards short of the first green, pitched to four feet and birdied, and three holes later had a chance to eagle the fourth. A drive and a marvellous six iron left him just eight feet from the cup, but he missed the putt for the 3 and settled for a birdie 4. Two under now, he drove with a four iron on the seventh and pitched to four feet, and followed with another birdie at the eighth. Furyk's eight iron ran

Vijay Singh (77) went two over after three.

Sam Torrance (78) started with two bogeys.

just off the green, but he holed out from 35 feet.

Out in 32, he began the home nine with a birdie 3 at the 11th — only three others birdied there this day — drilling a two iron to five feet.

Now Furyk stood five under par; seven more pars and he would shoot 66. He couldn't hold on. Poor drives cost him bogeys on the 13th and 18th, but he had one further birdie. Into the full force of the wind, he ripped a three iron to 20 feet on the 14th and holed the putt.

Relaxed now that the ordeal was over, Furyk said, "I really like this kind of golf. You need a lot of imagination, especially downwind. We're not used to landing the ball maybe 30 yards short of the green and letting it run to the hole."

On the other hand, Clarke had played under these conditions often. At age 28, a year older than Furyk, Clarke is about the same height but possibly 25 pounds heavier. He, too, went out in 32 with birdies on both the par-5 holes, where he hit ridiculous clubs for his second shots — a nine iron to the fourth and a five iron to the sixth. Both irons found bunkers, though, and Clarke had to save his birdies by holing from five feet on both holes.

He had begun his run of birdies by rolling in a putt from 20 feet on the second and added another from 25 feet on the seventh. He lost a stroke at the 10th, but like Furyk he birdied the 11th, reaching the green with a two iron and then holing an outrageous putt from perhaps 70 feet. He birdied the 16th as well, taking three strokes to reach the green and holing from 12 feet. Again like Furyk, he bogeyed the 18th by driving into the right rough.

As solidly as both Furyk and Clarke played that difficult homeward nine, no one's finish compared to Parnevik's. Jesper had matched par 36 going out and started back with a double-bogey 6 on the difficult 11th. He was still two over par after the 13th, but suddenly he began playing superb golf, birdied the 14th, lost a stroke on the 15th, then birdied the last three holes — four birdies in five holes. He came in with 70 and saved himself for greater challenges ahead.

There would be none for Ian Baker-Finch. He had won the Open at Royal Birkdale in 1991, but he simply could not play at this level any longer. He tried though, and he played badly. Out in 44, he stumbled home in 48 and shot 92. Despondent, he walked to the scorer's room to turn in his card and couldn't open the door.

In a mournful tone he said, "They've locked me out."

FIRST ROUND RESULTS

HOLE	1	2	3	4	5	6	7	8	9	10	11	12	13	14	15	16	17	18	
PAR	4	4	4	5	3	5	4	3	4	4	4	4	4	3	4	5	3	4	TOTAL
Jim Furyk	3	4	4	4	3	5	3	2	4	4	3	4	5	2	4	5	3	5	67
Darren Clarke	4	3	4	4	3	4	3	3	4	5	3	4	4	3	4	4	3	5	67
Greg Norman	4	4	3	4	4	4	3	3	3	4	4	4	5	3	4	5	3	5	69
Fred Couples	3	4	4	4	3	4	3	3	3	5	5	4	3	4	5	5	3	5	69
Justin Leonard	4	3	4	5	3	3	5	3	4	4	4	4	5	3	4	4	3	4	69
Angel Cabrera	3	5	4	4	3	4	4	4	4	3	4	3	6	3	4	5	3	4	70
Davis Love III	3	4	3	4	3	4	4	3	4	4	5	4	4	4	5	5	3	4	70
Andrew Magee	4	4	4	4	3	4	4	3	4	5	4	4	4	4	4	5	2	4	70
Jesper Parnevik	4	3	4	5	4	4	5	3	4	4	6	4	4	2	5	4	2	3	70
*Barclay Howard	3	3	4	4	3	4	4	3	4	5	5	3	5	3	4	5	3	5	70
Tom Watson	3	4	4	4	3	4	4	3	4	5	4	4	5	3	4	5	4	4	71
Ian Woosnam	5	4	5	4	4	4	4	2	3	4	5	4	5	3	4	4	3	4	71
David Tapping	3	4	4	4	3	5	4	3	4	4	4	5	5	3	3	5	3	5	71
Curtis Strange	3	4	4	5	3	5	4	3	4	4	4	4	4	2	5	5	3	5	71
Nick Faldo	4	5	4	4	3	4	4	3	5	5	4	4	4	3	4	5	3	3	71
Jay Haas	4	3	4	5	3	5	4	2	4	5	3	4	4	4	4	5	3	5	71

*Denotes amateur

HOLE SUMMARY

HOLE	PAR	EAGLES	BIRDIES	PARS	BOGEYS	HIGHER	RANK	AVERAGE
1	4	1	34	103	16	2	16	3.90
2	4	0	13	122	19	2	15	4.06
3	4	0	15	101	38	2	12	4.17
4	5	1	85	60	10	0	18	4.51
5	3	0	11	110	33	2	10	3.17
6	5	3	66	73	12	2	17	4.64
7	4	0	18	113	21	4	13	4.08
8	3	0	21	86	34	15	7	3.29
9	4	0	18	97	36	5	11	4.19
OUT	36	5	281	865	219	34		36.01
10	4	0	2	53	78	23	3	4.81
11	4	0	4	54	64	34	1	4.92
12	4	0	5	97	49	5	8	4.36
13	4	0	2	51	81	22	2	4.83
14	3	1	12	93	45	5	9	3.26
15	4	0	3	64	78	11	6	4.63
16	5	0	24	98	30	4	13	5.10
17	3	0	5	74	66	11	4	3.55
18	4	0	5	64	62	25	5	4.72
IN	35	1	62	648	553	140		40.18
TOTAL	71	6	343	1513	772	174		76.19

			LOW SCORES		
Players Below Par	10				
Players At Par	6		Low First Nine	Fred Couples	31
Players Above Par	140		Low Second Nine	Jesper Parnevik	34
			Low Round	Darren Clarke	67
				Jim Furyk	67

WEATHER

Fine and dry.
Brisk northwesterly wind.

Colin Montgomerie warned in advance of Royal Troon, "You're really hanging on from the seventh tee onward."

THE BEST OF LINKS GOLF

BY ROBERT GREEN

Just as it seems the Ryder Cup cannot be played these days without the phrase "golf is the winner" being invoked at least twice during the week — assuredly once at the beginning and once at the end — it could justifiably be argued that the victor on the first day of this year's Open Championship at Royal Troon did not appear in human form.

Notwithstanding the evident fact that no champion has ever been declared at the conclusion of the first round, the overwhelming presence on this occasion was that of the grand old links itself rather than co-leaders Darren Clarke and Jim Furyk, or the more celebrated duo of Greg Norman and Fred Couples, who shared third place with Justin Leonard.

As is invariably the case when a links course bares its teeth, it is with the indispensable assistance of the elements. And on Thursday, the wind emphatically arrived to torment the competitors with its caprices.

At 7,019 yards, Troon is hardly a pitch-and-putt course in the gentlest of circumstances. The par for its respective nines for this year's Open were 36 and 35, making for a par of 71 in all, compared to the 72 it had been in the recent past. This time around, the 11th, the notorious Railway hole, shed 18 yards in undergoing the metamorphosis from a relatively benign par-5 to a brutal par-4. "If a hole does not really play as a par-5, it should not be one," was the explanation of Angus Farquhar, the Championship Assistant. Reasonable enough, although the combination of the wind and the gorse meant the hole played as a par-7 for Tiger Woods on this day.

One of the inherent characteristics of a links is that the true par, like the relevance of yardages, frequently bears no relation to what is printed on the scorecard. If the effective par through the first day of this Open Championship was 71 — and only 10 players beat that total, so it constituted a pretty severe standard — then it was made up of something like 32 on the front nine and 39 on the back.

The northwesterly wind that blew at least 20 miles an hour for most of the day wasn't of the ferocity that reportedly landed some fish on the fourth green during a particularly vigorous blow in 1952, but it was sufficient for Nick Faldo to say, "It was as tough as I have played a links for moons."

To suggest the Ayrshire coastline bears a significant resemblance to the lunar landscape would be stretching fantasy a little too far, although one competitor's golf was out of this world over the dauntingly tough final five holes.

Jesper Parnevik had reached the turn in 36 and then double-bogeyed the 11th. Two over par at that point, he birdied the 14th, 16th, 17th and 18th, and even though he bogeyed the 15th, that turned a likely 75 into a 70.

Perhaps no competitor at this year's championship was better qualified to comment on the conditions than three-time winner, 57-year-old Jack Nicklaus, returning for the fourth time to the scene of his debut in the championship in 1962. "There were about six par-5s on the back nine," he said, "holes I could not reach in two shots. The 12th is the only realistic par-4." By way of example, Nicklaus hit two drivers to the 10th, which measures 438 yards, and he needed to hit a nine iron for his *third* shot at both the 13th (465 yards, no bunkers and with a fairway badly in need of ironing) and 15th (not much easier). He shot 35 coming home, the official par, albeit he said, "Par for the back nine today is 39 or 40." Jack only shot his personal four or five under because he holed a bunker shot on the 16th, the only hole coming home that the scorecard considered a par-5.

Faldo, who went into this Open with a career record of 33 rounds below 70, a mark that matched Nicklaus' record, hit a two iron to 18 feet at the last for a closing birdie and a round of 71. He was then keen to point out that playing downwind isn't necessarily a picnic either.

Greg Norman said he welcomed the wind.

"It's not so easy when it's howling downwind as it might seem," Faldo said. "You have to judge your shots really well. It's a weird feeling trying to land a wedge short. I bogeyed the second hole because I was too close to the hole. I had a shot from about 80 yards and I didn't have a club for it."

Woods provided ample evidence of the problems. On the first hole, which measured 364 yards, his eagerly awaited drive bounded into the front left-hand bunker at such speed that, according to Brad Faxon, who was in the group ahead putting out on the hole, it would have run through the green by many yards had the sand not impeded its progress. As jestingly suggested in some quarters, Tiger was close to being on the second hole before he had completed the first. In fact, Woods then hit his trap shot into another bunker beyond the green. He had failed to make due allowance for the wind.

Davis Love III amplified the problems of practising for such conditions, having hit a five iron 275 yards going out and then hit one a mere 149 yards on the inward nine. "You try to practise these shots when you get here, but it's hard to practise," he said. "There's no such thing as a stock nine iron out there today. You're not going to hit a nine iron 140 yards,

no matter which way you're going."

Greg Norman, as if tempting the fates, welcomed the weather. "I've always felt the British Open hasn't had enough wind in the last couple of years," he said. On the long 16th, Norman hit his two iron 165 yards, and he hit it well. On the 17th, he went with a three wood — and how often do you see a tournament professional with a wood in his hands on a par-3 — but he could have hauled out the driver. "It was 230 yards to the back of the green, and if you just hit a solid driver, you're not going to hit it over that green."

The recently crowned US Open champion, Ernie Els, even felt sympathy for his less powerful peers. "The 18th is a real struggle to reach the fairway," he confessed. "All you can see is rough from the tee; maybe it's a little unfair." His parting shot was an almost wistful, "Geez, this game can drive you insane sometimes."

Justin Leonard would have agreed with Els. His drive at the last was, he estimated, "10 or 15 yards short of the fairway. I could see the people walking across the fairway kind of almost sniggering. I guess maybe we are brought down to a level they're accustomed to." Most handicap golfers could relate to Leonard's back nine. Playing it strictly by the book, he didn't hit a single green in regulation. From there on, the analogy collapses like an old souffle. Leonard played the back nine in 35.

"I used the one iron from most of the tees on the front and for most of my second shots on the back," Leonard said. Another difference. Most handicap golfers can't hit a one iron in any circumstances. Echoing what Love had said, Tom Watson, five times a winner of the Open and the champion at Troon in 1982, volunteered that on the front nine he was hitting his one iron 280 yards and on the back only 190. With no wind, he would be looking for 225.

In all, the conditions conspired to bring out the best in links golf. No one wants to see championship golf contested in the rain, which in fact hardly affects the professionals since they have caddies to keep their grips dry and a limitless supply of new gloves. In fact, since the rain slows down the greens and reduces the likelihood of unpredictable bounces, wet-

Nick Faldo and Nick Price were among the stars unsuccessfully battling the winds of the first round.

weather golf is actually quite a favourable prospect for them.

Troon this Thursday had it right. The morning was overcast, the air cold, the wind strong. But it was fine. In the afternoon, the sun broke through, speeding up the course and brightening up the scene.

As Norman explained, addressing the issue of why links golf is so different and so rewarding, "You only get conditions like this at the British Open. You may get them sometimes in Australia, because our conditions get very windy, very hard and very fast out there, but our golf courses aren't like links courses; so nowhere else in the world do you get to savour this. You've got to imagine shots, you've got to picture shots you want to hit, and you've got to execute them. And you don't get to practise a lot of them. I mean, I took 37 shots on the back nine. There's probably 15 of those that I don't practise."

Links golf offers a wide range of choices, sometimes a plethora. If you have 100 yards to a flag and there's a large pond between you and the hole, the only way to hit the shot is through the air. On a links, that would be one option, but you might instead choose to play a low pitch that hits the ground before the green, and the club you use to play the shot will dictate how much the ball flies through the air and how much it runs along the ground. You've got to invent shots; in Norman's words, you have to imagine shots. The degree of versatility and ability *demanded* of the player on a links, as opposed to the number of alternative strategies he has at his discretion, is largely dictated by the strength of the wind. That was the case at Royal Troon. As the American Ryder Cup captain, Tom Kite, put it, "No matter how well you scored, you got beat up." And he had a 72.

Colin Montgomerie has been Europe's leading money-winner for the past four seasons. He is also arguably the best golfer currently playing who has yet to win a major championship. Furthermore, he is a native of Troon. His father, James, is the club's Secretary. Before the championship, being more aware than most of the potential terrors posed by the prevailing wind, he told *Golf Digest*, "You're really hanging on from the seventh tee onward."

On this Thursday, Monty was two under par after six holes. And his words, unfortunately, were to prove prophetic. He shot 76. But while Montgomerie might have lost out this time, golf — I'm afraid to say — was the winner.

Darren Clarke (133) shot 66 playing intelligent golf. He said, "As soon as you go into bunkers here it's a penalty shot."

CLARKE STANDS TWO AHEAD

BY ROBERT SOMMERS

In his last full year as an amateur, Darren Clarke won the North of Ireland Amateur, the South of Ireland Amateur, the Irish Closed Amateur and the Spanish Amateur. He didn't lose a tournament all year. He played with great confidence, consistency and elan and came to the PGA European Tour with so much talent he nearly guaranteed immediate success.

Assumptions of this sort don't always work out. Somehow he lost his consistency and along with it his confidence. The shots that once flew arrow-straight to their target somehow veered off line, and instead of putting for birdie, he was putting for survival. Rudderless, he lost faith in himself, and he foundered. Even though others told him how good he could be, he didn't believe it.

It took Clarke, now 28 years of age, three years to win his first tournament in 1993 and three more to win his second. Now, after shooting 66 in the second round, he stood in position to win the Open Championship. With 133 for 36 holes, three strokes above Nick Faldo's record 130 of 1992, he stood two strokes ahead of the field halfway through this gruelling test of skill and character.

Justin Leonard, Jesper Parnevik and David Tapping shot 66s as well. Leonard climbed into second place, at 135; Parnevik moved into third, at 136, and Tapping, a 22-year-old Englishman playing in his first Open, tied for fourth, at 137, with Fred Couples who held his ground with 68.

Tom Lehman, meanwhile, fell further behind by shooting 72 and dropping 13 strokes behind Clarke. Jim Furyk, who had shared the first-round lead with Clarke, shot 72 as well and fell six strokes behind, and Greg Norman shot 73 and dropped from two behind to nine back.

Under a bright sun and only a moderate breeze, Royal Troon had lost much of its sting; it was still tough, although less impossible. No one complained they couldn't reach the fairways with well-played shots, and the scoring reflected the easier conditions. Just 10 men had shot under par 71 in the first round, but 45 broke par in the second round. Where 140 had shot 72 or higher in the first round, only 92 failed to match par in the second.

Five men shot 66, five others shot 67, seven shot 68, and 13 more shot 69. It was quite a change, and it helped a number of players. Never comfortable in the wind, Colin Montgomerie rebounded from his grim opening 76 with 69. Tom Kite moved among the leaders with 67. Mark James shot 67 as well, and so did Mark Calcavecchia, Brad Faxon and Mark McNulty.

Ernie Els made a slight move upward with 69, but it wasn't enough. Faldo couldn't hole any kind of putt and shot a dull 73, and Nick Price, who had been doing so well lately, shot 78 and missed the cut.

In the midst of the day's developments, Dennis Edlund and Daniel Olsson, both from Sweden, holed in one, Edlund at the eighth and Olsson at the fifth. Another Swede, Pierre Fulke, holed in one on the 14th in the first round after having made another at Loch Lomond the previous week. Other than the thrill of it, they did no good for either man; they all missed the 36-hole cut.

Clarke, on the other hand, had no such thoughts. Among the early starters, going off a few minutes after 8 o'clock, he raced through the first nine in 32, running off six birdies but losing strokes on each of the par-3 holes where he missed the greens. He played just as well coming back, but the severe demands of Troon's closing holes asked for much more than the outward nine. Even so, Clarke played first-rate golf, and except for a bogey on the 10th, he hit the middle of nearly every green.

His putting was immaculate. He had come to Troon unsure of his stroke, but he solved his inconsistency by shortening his backstroke to avoid mak-

David Tapping (137) had a surprising 66.

ing contact on the upswing, and changing to another putter he had in reserve. With his new method he stroked only 28 putts. Five times he holed from 20 feet, and he made one from 10 feet and another from eight. His other birdie came on the fourth, the first of the par-5s, where he reached the green with a three-wood second and two-putted from 40 feet.

Clarke had been given a tutorial in how to play Troon from Montgomerie, who grew up in the town. His father, James Montgomerie, had been Secretary of the Royal Troon Golf Club for a number of years and Colin knew the course intimately.

Speaking of their practice rounds together, Clarke said Montgomerie emphasized where not to go, what shots not to take, the safest side to miss on, and where the R and A would probably cut the holes. He said Montgomerie gave him a lot of good advice that he felt was worth several strokes.

Clarke evidently learned his lessons well. Going out he holed from 20 feet on the first, 10 feet on the second, and from 20 feet on the seventh and ninth. Four under par now, he hit his drive into the right rough on the 10th and missed the green, but played rock steady the rest of the way in, holing from 20 feet again on the 14th and once more on the 16th, the last of the par-5s.

Justin Leonard (135) pitched to close range at the 12th.

Jesper Parnevik (136) said after his 66 that the Open "is the only tournament that makes your hair stand on end."

Fred Couples (137) shot 68 by saving par from a bunker at the 17th and birdieing the 18th.

Tom Kite (139) was delighted by the weather.

Brad Faxon (144) came back with 67.

Jim Furyk (139) slipped to a 72 but said, "I didn't shoot myself in the foot. I'm still in contention."

He might have shot 65, but after a stunning iron to the 18th, perhaps his best of the day, he missed a putt from little more than four feet for the birdie. With a par 4, he still shot 66 and waited for the rest of the field to catch up, if they could.

Clarke had played intelligent, mature golf, eliminating risk when he could. For example, had he used his driver he might have driven the greens of the first two holes, but he might also have found bunkers. "As soon as you go into bunkers here it's a penalty shot," he explained. "There's no going forward; just get it out."

Instead, he drove with a four iron on the first and a three iron on the second, stayed short of the bunkers, and birdied both holes. He was also encouraged by Steve Jones, the 1996 US Open champion. Clarke explained that, "Every time I holed a putt he would say, 'Come on, one more.'"

Clarke had hardly been in for half an hour when Parnevik started home with a 66 of his own to climb within three strokes of him with half the championship still to be played. As everyone knows, Parnevik loves the Open. He says, "It is pretty much the only

tournament that makes your hair stand on end."

He is also one of life's eccentrics, who does strange things with both his body and his equipment. Every month or so he purges himself with a diet of treated volcanic sand, which he believes, "cleans out the mercury you can get from eating fish." Beside mercury, the latest dose obviously flushed away whatever bad golf might have infected his system, because he played mostly good shots this day.

Even stranger, perhaps, Jesper had putted sublimely in birdieing three of the last four holes of the first round, but he wasn't satisfied. "My game and my putting felt terrible," he said, and so he changed to a new putter with a rubber insert on the face. Then he hit his first putt 12 feet past the hole and bogeyed the first.

That was his last mistake, except for a wild drive on the 18th. He hit every green except the last, and he eagled the fourth after a three iron to six feet, which made up for the bogey on the first. He birdied both the seventh and eighth with fine pitch shots to eight feet and six feet and went out in 33.

After holing from 25 feet for another birdie on the

41

With birdies on the first two holes, Tom Watson (141) shot 70 but said he wasn't yet thinking of a sixth Open title.

Generally-steady Jay Haas (141) had 70 to move into a tie for ninth place.

difficult 11th, Parnevik played routine pars to the 16th, where he hooked his second shot badly. Never mind; from the rough he lofted a pitch to less than three feet and birdied again.

He did indeed look as if he would lose a stroke on the 18th, where he drove so wildly his ball lay behind a grandstand 200 yards from the green. Using an eight iron for the loft he needed, he hit his second into a pot bunker 30 yards short of the green, followed with a sand iron that he hit as hard as he could, and felt lucky to reach the front edge of the green, 50 feet from the hole. The putt he faced was not easy. Jesper claimed it had 15 feet of break, but it showed that Parnevik knew exactly what he was doing when he changed putters. He rolled his ball dead into the cup for the par 4. Back in 33, he had his 66.

Talking of the round later, Parnevik confessed that, "If you take the game too seriously it will drive you mad, as a lot of other golfers have noticed. It is the most frustrating game you can try, and a very tough one to play for a living."

Clarke and Parnevik had finished long before Leonard teed off, just after 2 o'clock, and he knew what he needed to stay afloat. Not much had been expected from him when the Open began. Some felt

Mark James (143) posted a second-round 67.

Jose Maria Olazabal (143) recovered with his 68.

Davis Love III (141) stayed close to the leaders.

Angel Cabrera (140) recorded a second 70.

he didn't have the game for this level of competition, even though he had won twice since he joined the USPGA Tour in 1994.

In tough conditions the previous day, Leonard had played the first nine in 34. Now, with the wind eased, he went out in 31 with one bogey, two birdies and, for the first time since his amateur days, two eagles. Even without the full force of the previous day's blow, he was on both the fourth and the sixth greens with five-iron second shots and holed both, from 15 feet on the fourth, and from 20 feet on the sixth. He had birdied the second from 12 feet and bogeyed the fifth by missing the green, so now he stood four under par. An eight-iron pitch nearly rattled the cup on the seventh and he holed again from a foot or so.

Now he turned for the long fight back to the old grey clubhouse knowing he would have to play strong, steady golf to make his par 35. He lost a stroke on the dreaded 11th, but he had some luck on the 13th. From a good lie in the fairway he played a low three iron that bored through the wind toward the distant green. Leonard frowned when he saw his

The 1989 Open champion, Mark Calcavecchia (141) shot a second-round 67 for a share of ninth place.

ball head left of the green, but he switched to a slight smile when it bounced off a little mound and rolled within 20 feet of the cup. He holed it, birdied the 16th with a 20-yard pitch to four feet, and after a steady par 3 at the 17th, needed only a 4 on the 18th for 65.

He played it well, hitting his four iron about 40 feet from the cup, but perhaps too eager for another birdie, he rammed his first putt six feet past the hole and missed coming back.

Asked about his two eagles, Leonard grinned and said, "Remember I had eagled the sixth yesterday. When I stood over my ball on the fourth today I thought, if you hit such a good shot in here it would be nice to take advantage of it. When I got to the sixth I thought, 'You just eagled the fourth, but big deal,' and I knocked the putt in."

As Leonard made his big move, Mickelson and Woods were heading nowhere. On the brink of missing the cut after his opening 76, Mickelson saved himself with 68, only his third round in the 60s in his five Opens. He had shot 67 as an amateur in 1991 and 69 in the last round at Royal Lytham in 1996.

Nick Faldo (144) fell further behind with 73.

Despite an outstanding year until now, Steve Elkington (148) missed the 36-hole cut by one stroke.

Tiger Woods (146) struggled for par on the 16th.

Woods, meantime, played erratic golf once again. On a course where the best players feed on the first nine, Tiger shot even-par 36 with two birdies and two bogeys. His round collapsed completely when he overshot the 10th green. With his ball lying close to a gorse bush, Woods tried to chop it onto the green, but his wedge hit a branch of the bush and the clubhead slipped under the ball, moving it perhaps an inch or two. Next he dug at it again and still left it short, and before he calmed himself, he quickly swiped at the ball and knocked it over the green.

Seeing Woods' rising anger, his caddie rushed to the ball and placed the bag next to it so that Tiger couldn't play another careless, impetuous shot. Woods made an 8, four over par, and finished the day with 74, dropping into a tie for 49th place with, among others, defending champion Tom Lehman, who had his own sad story to tell.

Lehman hit the ball only five times on the second hole, which is enough, but he walked off with a 7 on his scorecard. After his first putt, he had moved his ball one putter-head length off Vijay Singh's line, but he had been distracted when he found a cut in his ball and forgot to replace it on the proper spot.

Something strange happened then. No one had noticed the mistake, but as the group left the third tee, Lehman saw Tim Taylor, the rules official as-

Robert Damron (149) was among the US newcomers.

Amateur champion Craig Watson (149) missed the cut.

signed to the grouping, leafing through the rules book. Thinking back to what he might have done on the second green, Lehman suddenly realised he had putted from the wrong place.

Lehman assumed he would be disqualified, but when he approached Taylor and explained what had happened, he was assured he was still in the championship but that he should add two strokes to his score. Strangely, Taylor hadn't noticed the violation; he was looking in the rules book to satisfy himself about another matter.

Lehman, though, was angry, both at himself and at his caddie. "If I had been disqualified I would have had an embarrassing walk in," he said. "I'm mad at myself and my caddie."

At least he qualified for the last two rounds, though. The 36-hole cut fell at 147 and eliminated two of the Open's finest champions of the past — Seve Ballesteros and Gary Player, each of whom won three Opens.

Never playing close to his best golf, Steve Elkington missed the cut by one stroke. Price went out as well, along with Lee Janzen, Craig Stadler, Amateur champion Craig Watson, Costantino Rocca, Mark Brooks, the 1996 USPGA champion, John Cook, who came so close at Muirfield in 1992, Sam Torrance, Sandy Lyle, the 1985 champion, and Paul Azinger.

Gary Player (149) shot 71 in the second round.

SECOND ROUND RESULTS

HOLE	1	2	3	4	5	6	7	8	9	10	11	12	13	14	15	16	17	18	
PAR	4	4	4	5	3	5	4	3	4	4	4	4	4	3	4	5	3	4	TOTAL
Darren Clarke	3	3	4	4	4	4	3	4	3	5	4	4	4	2	4	4	3	4	66-133
Justin Leonard	4	4	3	4	3	3	3	4	4	5	4	3	3	4	4	3	5		66-135
Jesper Parnevik	5	4	4	3	3	5	3	2	4	3	4	4	3	4	4	4	3	4	66-136
Fred Couples	3	4	4	4	3	5	4	3	4	4	4	4	4	3	4	5	3	3	68-137
David Tapping	4	3	4	5	3	4	4	2	4	3	3	5	4	3	3	5	3	4	66-137
Jim Furyk	4	4	4	6	3	5	5	2	4	4	4	5	4	3	4	4	3	4	72-139
Tom Kite	3	4	4	4	4	4	4	3	3	5	3	4	3	3	4	5	3	4	67-139
Angel Cabrera	5	4	4	5	4	5	3	2	3	4	5	3	5	3	4	4	3	4	70-140
Jay Haas	4	4	4	4	3	4	4	2	3	5	4	5	3	5	5	5	3	4	70-141
Tom Watson	3	3	4	5	3	4	3	4	4	5	4	5	3	3	5	4	3	5	70-141
Mark Calcavecchia	3	4	3	4	3	5	4	3	4	5	4	5	3	2	4	5	3	3	67-141
Davis Love III	5	4	4	4	3	4	3	4	4	5	4	4	4	3	4	5	3	4	71-141

HOLE SUMMARY

HOLE	PAR	EAGLES	BIRDIES	PARS	BOGEYS	HIGHER	RANK	AVERAGE
1	4	0	29	109	13	1	16	3.91
2	4	0	28	107	15	2	13	3.95
3	4	0	27	107	18	0	14	3.94
4	5	10	64	68	9	1	18	4.52
5	3	1	15	104	31	1	8	3.11
6	5	3	56	78	13	2	17	4.70
7	4	0	28	101	20	3	11	3.99
8	3	1	31	89	27	4	10	3.05
9	4	0	25	104	22	1	11	3.99
OUT	36	15	303	867	168	15		35.16
10	4	0	7	73	63	9	2	4.51
11	4	0	7	77	55	13	1	4.54
12	4	0	17	103	30	2	9	4.11
13	4	0	16	96	39	1	6	4.16
14	3	0	17	105	27	3	6	3.12
15	4	0	8	93	46	5	4	4.32
16	5	0	33	103	12	4	15	4.91
17	3	0	8	101	35	8	3	3.30
18	4	0	12	90	44	6	5	4.29
IN	35	0	125	841	351	51		37.26
TOTAL	71	15	428	1708	519	66		72.42

Players Below Par	45
Players At Par	15
Players Above Par	92

WEATHER

Dry and sunny.
Light wind from the northwest.

LOW SCORES

Low First Nine	Robert Allenby	31
	David Howell	31
	Justin Leonard	31
	Colin Montgomerie	31
Low Second Nine	Mark James	33
	Jesper Parnevik	33
	David Tapping	33
Low Round	Darren Clarke	66
	Justin Leonard	66
	Jesper Parnevik	66
	David Tapping	66

Tiger Woods said the course was severe "because of the undulations in the fairway ... But I love to be able to play creatively. The short game is brought back into play. You don't just hit a wedge every time you miss a green."

COMMENTARY

TROON PLAYS NO FAVOURITES

BY ANDREW FARRELL

Can there be a better feeling than waking up to a glorious day at the Scottish seaside, knowing the midsummer sun has been up for hours and when only the day before you were cursing your luck and the inclement British weather? The forecast had been for Thursday's wind to continue all week, which should have been the clue.

Friday dawned with nary a breath to ripple the Firth of Clyde. The isles of Arran and Bute shimmered in the heat haze. How could you not have fun out on the links on a morning like this? If there was still something hanging in the air, it was this niggling question: What had gone wrong with the 126th Open Championship?

Don't get me wrong. With three days to go, the championship still present mystifying possibilities and intrigue, some old characters and many new ones to watch and talk about and write about. But already, it seemed, the Open was not going to live up to its pre-publicity. It was a tall order, since the essence of the build-up was that this was to be the greatest shoot-out of top names the game had ever seen. Well, it never does to underplay these things, does it?

Arriving at Royal Troon was not just one of the best fields to compete in a major championship, but one where the best players were in their best form. "Every man and his dog is here this week," Ernie Els said. "It looks like everybody is playing well, so it is going to be a really interesting week."

Els had got the ball rolling by winning a thrilling US Open only a month before. Throughout the final round at Congressional, Els battled against Tom Lehman, Colin Montgomerie and Jeff Maggert before beating Montgomerie by one stroke and Lehman by two. For an encore, Els won the Buick Classic for the second year running from start to finish the following week.

The double-header put Els on top of the World Ranking for the first time, but his stay was short-lived. Greg Norman, whose record 96-week run as No. 1 had come to an end earlier in the year, won the FedEx St Jude Classic by birdieing the last three holes, to regain the top spot. It was Norman's first USPGA Tour victory of the year, so it was a good time for the two-time Open champion to be finding his form.

It took only another week for the crown of the best player in the world to change again. Tiger Woods, already the youngest winner of the US Masters, had become, at 21 years of age, the most youthful world No. 1 in June, and his victory at the Motorola Western Open put him back where he seems destined to stay for much of his career.

It was Woods' fourth win on the USPGA Tour in 1997, his fifth anywhere and seventh of his professional career, which was less than a year old. It put him on course to become the first player to break $2 million in a season on the Tour and quashed talk of a "slump". Prior to the Western, Woods had only broken 70 once in his previous 11 rounds. All it had taken was a week with his feet up to recharge his power.

On the same weekend but on the other side of the Atlantic, Montgomerie was retaining his Murphy's Irish Open title at Druids Glen. The Scot had won the Compaq European Grand Prix before his narrow defeat at the US Open, but this surpassed anything he had done before. In a closing round of 62, two inside the course record, the Scot came from three behind the rising star Lee Westwood to win by seven. "I can honestly say," he said, "I have never been playing better going into an Open."

Tom Lehman had cause to say much the same, as he returned with the silver claret jug, when he won the Gulfstream Loch Lomond World Invitational. The American had a 19-under-par total of 265 on a course designed by Tom Weiskopf and Jay Morrish which is reckoned to be one of the best in the coun-

Colin Montgomerie said, "Golf comes and goes."

try. He won by five strokes from Els, who with Mark McCumber had been runner-up in the Open to Lehman at Royal Lytham the year before.

All the players had caught the mood, but only Lehman qualified his enthusiasm. "It really doesn't happen very often that all the best players are playing well at one time," he said. "But what would be really exciting would be for all the guys who are supposedly in good form to still be in good form on Sunday."

By Friday, we knew that was not going to happen. Thursday's wind had seen to that. "Everyone has been talking whether the golf ball goes too far these days," said Peter Greenhough, Chairman of the R and A's Championship Committee. "But when you get a true links course with true links weather, even the best players find it difficult." The best of the quintet in the first round had been Norman with a 69.

The Australian would not shoot better all week. The problem was his putting. Friday was typical. Having seen none of his other top rivals take advantage of the easier conditions to make a run at the leader, Darren Clarke, Norman struggled to a 73 with one one-putt and 17 two-putts. "That doesn't

get the job done in these tournaments," observed the Australian. His frustration would get no better as he closed with rounds of 70 and 75.

Most expectation, of course, centred on Woods. In theory, he was meant to be able to overpower the front nine and use his length to cope with the 3,650-yard, par-35 back nine while others struggled. In order to combat the wind, Woods had been working on a shallower swing in practice to lower his ball flight. While the two par-5s on the front nine, the fourth and the sixth, were virtually "gimme" birdies for Woods all week, he only went to the turn in the first round in 35. "He tried to attack the golf course," said Michael Bonallack, the R and A Secretary. "He got into all sorts of trouble. He'll learn."

While Woods hit a 435-yard drive at the fourth, when he tried to drive the green at the 402-yard dogleg seventh, he found a greenside bunker and only came out with a par. Meantime, back into the wind, his approach to the last was from 165 yards with a four iron. Such is links golf. You learn the hard way, as Woods did at the Railway, the 11th hole. He drove into a bush, took an unplayable lie, tried a two iron from the rough but caught a mound, then went over the green with an eight iron and failed to get up and down. A triple-bogey 7, although two birdies in his last three holes gave him 72, well below the day's average.

Without the wind, what would he do? Much the same, as it turned out. Speaking of his length, Woods said, "Yes, it is an advantage, but only if I hit the fairway." Fairway seemed to be an endangered species at Troon this year, and the rough was long and lush. In practice, when Woods missed the first fairway, a local had growled, "You'll nae turn this course into a pitch-and-putt."

Bogeys at the third and fifth meant Woods was out in level par, and this time his disaster occurred at the 10th. This one cost a quadruple-bogey 8. His three wood from the blind tee caught the left rough, from where his eight iron caught a flier and went over the green against a gorse bush. His first thrash went completely under the ball, his second moved it six yards into a position that was not much better, and his next put the ball over the front of the green.

Playing the last eight holes in one under, for 74, was quite an achievement.

Woods ended the second day 13 strokes off the lead. He reminded us that he was further behind when he charged back to lose by only one to Mark O'Meara at the AT&T Pebble Beach National Pro-Am. On Saturday, he was finally to show us what he could do, matching Greg Norman's course-record 64, but on Sunday he was back in the old routine. A triple-bogey 6 at the Postage Stamp, the eighth, meant a third disaster. "I had three bad holes, which you musn't let happen, but the week was not all bad," he said. "I look forward to coming over here. I have always been determined to win the British Open. It is the one with the most tradition and it would mean a lot to me."

Lehman can tell him how much. The 38-year-old former mini-tour player found great comfort in seeing the Open trophy on his mantelpiece every time he returned from a tournament, but after an opening 74, an incident on the second green on Friday confirmed he was not to have that pleasure for a second year. It also epitomised this most decent of men. Lehman forgot to replace his ball marker, something no one else had seen, and owned up when he realised walking down the third fairway.

"I have never done anything dumb like that before," he said. "I thought I would be disqualified and how embarrassing it would be walking in from there." It was actually a two-shot penalty, added to a bogey, and Lehman was so mad he made up the three strokes on the rest of the front nine. But his 72 meant he was too far off the pace, and after another 72 on Saturday, he finished on a high with a 66. He was warmly applauded up the last.

Els closed with three consecutive rounds of 69, but had started with a 75. "That's when I played myself out of it," he said. "The rhythm of my swing just did not feel comfortable." A double-bogey 6 at the 10th was the prelude for a back nine of 40. "It is always difficult going for back-to-back majors, however well you are playing," he added.

As for Montgomerie, he had started the week by receiving the Association of Golf Writers' Trophy for achieving a fourth consecutive Order of Merit win in

Greg Norman's problem was his putting.

1996. He spoke well, describing how he had struck his first shots as a golfer only a few yards from the tent where the dinner was being held.

He was a member of the club until he turned professional in 1987, but was offered honorary membership in 1996. His father, James, retired as Secretary shortly after the championship after 10 years in the job, and his wife, Eimear, was born in the town. "My best result ever in Troon," Montgomerie said, "was marrying my wife."

Montgomerie had played hundreds of rounds on the course, but the reason he was tipped as a contender was because of his straight hitting. Suddenly, during Wednesday's practice round, it deserted him. On Thursday, he only hit three fairways in a 76, and he managed only one more the following day. Rounds of 69 and 70 meant he finished joint 24th with Woods and Lehman. "This place is special for me and always will be," he said. "I look forward to when the Open comes round here again in seven or eight years."

He added, "Golf comes and goes. Favourites in golf are not always favourites. You can almost always pick the semi-finalists at Wimbledon, but golf is a different kettle of fish altogether."

No one played the second nine as well as Jesper Parnevik (202), who birdied the 10th with a 15-foot putt.

PARNEVIK CLIMBS INTO THE LEAD

BY ROBERT SOMMERS

Once before a golfer had led an Open Championship a Troon with a score of 133, which Darren Clarke had matched through his first two rounds. Even a five-stroke lead didn't assure victory, though. Instead it led to absolute collapse.

When Bobby Clampett opened the 1982 championship with 67 and 66 and played the first five holes of the third round in one under par, the gallery and the Press were ready to concede him the championship. His birdie on the fifth had been his 15th in the 41 holes he had played. He had gone 12 under par and opened a gaping seven-stroke lead over Des Smyth and had moved eight strokes ahead of young Nick Price and Tom Watson.

Clampett had played such mechanically perfect golf that he shocked everyone when his game turned sour on the sixth hole, the second of the par-5s. He butchered it. He pulled his drive into a fairway bunker and took dangerous risks trying to avoid losing one stroke. He caught the lip trying to play too long a recovery and went into another bunker, caught the lip again and moved his ball about 30 yards, pulled his fourth into rough, hit his fifth fat and into a greenside bunker, reached the green with his sixth and two-putted for an 8. Instead of losing one stroke, he lost three and with it the championship. Clampett shot 78 that day and 77 the next and gradually faded from championship golf. Watson won the Open, the fourth of his five.

Now Clarke had shot the same scores for the first 36 holes and looked directly into the eyes of the Clampett Curse. At the same time, he was looking into the eyes of yet another jinx. Fifty years had passed since the last Irishman had won the Open Championship. Fred Daly, a short, round man from Belfast, shot 293 at Hoylake and won the 1947 championship by one stroke over Reg Horne and Frank Stranahan.

Clarke might have whipped one hex, but he couldn't beat two; they ruined him, along with a multitude of loose shots on the homeward nine. He played the first nine well enough, going out in 32, but he lost the magic on the second, came home in a fumbling 39 when he needed something better, and with 71 fell from two strokes ahead to two strokes behind. Jesper Parnevik shot another 66 and jumped into the lead at 202. Clarke followed with 204, and Justin Leonard and Fred Couples were at 207. Couples shot 70 and Leonard a shaky 72.

Jim Furyk hung around the edges with 70 and 209, the same total as Stephen Ames and Eduardo Romero; and Tiger Woods finally played as everyone knew he could and shot 64, equalling the course record, the best round of the championship and one stroke higher than the Open record of 63, shared by seven men.

Once again it was a lovely day. Troon basked under a cobalt sky broken only by a milky white cloud bank in the distance. The sun sparkled on the Clyde estuary, and off shore a lone sailboat sought the wind that would carry her to harbour. Barely a puff rippled the calm sea, hardly enough to influence the flight of a golf ball. Troon hardly ever offered such invitations to scoring.

The players took advantage of the conditions. Of the 70 men who had survived the 36-hole eliminations, 29 shot under Royal Troon's par of 71 and five others matched it, one less than half the field. Besides Woods' 64, Parnevik, Ames and Robert Allenby shot 66s, Romero and Lee Westwood shot 67s, and Stuart Appleby, Frank Nobilo, Steve Jones and David Russell shot 68s. Eight men shot 69s, among them a second straight by Colin Montgomerie, which boosted him to 214, one over par and 12 strokes behind Parnevik, far too many to make up.

A number of other old as well as new heroes had the same prospects. Tom Watson, still a wonderful tee-to-green player, shot 70, and with 211 had nine

Fred Couples (207), who saved par here at the 12th, said, "I did not make any putts early on, then I struggled."

Justin Leonard (207) didn't putt as well as he had.

strokes to make up. Both Greg Norman and Curtis Strange shot 70s for 212, and Ian Woosnam, Phil Mickelson and Ernie Els each shot 69 and stood at 213, level par.

Jose Maria Olazabal, though, shot 73. Nick Faldo, playing worse every day, shot 75, which left him 17 strokes out of first place. Cheered every step he took, Jack Nicklaus shot 71, and with 218 tied for 27th place. Tom Lehman shot another 72, effectively ending whatever hopes he might have had to repeat.

Lehman had become a favourite of the galleries. They warmed to his modesty, and even a few mishaps with the silver claret jug that symbolizes the Open Championship were treated with mild amusement. Once his children dented it and once the police were called to apprehend a woman seen carrying it at 1 o'clock in the morning. She was innocent; Lehman had been to a party celebrating his winning the Open and asked her to take it to his office.

His warm and friendly manner charmed the public. On an early trip to Troon to assess the golf course, he had gone to dinner at a well-known restaurant. Recognizing him, the owner asked if Lehman would allow him to take his photograph. Lehman agreed but then said he had a better photograph at his hotel, then left and returned in 15 minutes with it.

Darren Clarke (204) had reason to smile at the 17th after his par-saving 20-foot putt.

Stephen Ames (209) came back in 32 for his 66.

Eduardo Romero (209) shot 67 after bogeying the 18th.

Because of incidents like these, the spectators willed him on, but Tom just didn't have his game this week. Nevertheless, even though he played loose golf and indifferent shots, they applauded and cheered him on every green.

Their cheers for Lehman, however, didn't approach the frenzy around Woods, arriving for his 11 o'clock starting time intending to attack the course.

"Basically, I had to shoot real low," Woods said. "Being so far back when I started, I had to do it. I've hit the ball real well the last two days, but I got nothing out of it, so I said that if I could eliminate those high-scoring holes I would be all right. That's about what happened."

He began by birdieing three of the first four holes, the first with a pitch inside two feet and the second by holing a 25-foot putt. Another birdie at the fourth, scored with an eight-iron second following another tremendous drive, and two putts from 30 feet. It was his third birdie there in three rounds.

A seven iron that flew over the green and two putts from six feet had cost him a bogey 4 at the fifth hole. He went to four under par with birdies at the sixth and the seventh, even though his somewhat wild drive at the second flew into the gallery and hit a

young girl. The ball rebounded into play, and Woods lofted a sand wedge 12 feet below the hole and ran it in. A missed 12-footer on the eighth cost him a birdie.

When he made the turn in 32, still four under par, Woods had fought back to level par for the championship. He couldn't relax yet, because now he had come to the heart of the golf course, the tortuous 3,650 yards of the second nine. He nearly lost one stroke on the 10th where his seven-iron approach kicked down off the side of a hill, down a slope and into the gallery, but he pitched to eight feet and saved his par 4.

The 11th cost him once again. He had made a 7 there in the first round, and now he drove into the gorse as he had then. He found his ball playable, but the prickly bushes cut into his back so badly he put on his caddie's windshirt for protection. More comfortable now, he hit a poor wedge into more gorse. At that point Woods appeared headed for another 7 or perhaps 8. Luckily, though, his ball sat in grass clear of the bushes, and he had a shot to the green. Another sand wedge braked four feet from the cup and he holed the putt. A bogey 5 where anything might have been possible. This was the kind of bogey

Robert Allenby (210) shot 68 and said, "I think I'm in contention provided the leaders don't go crazy."

Despite two bogeys, Tiger Woods (210) recorded a 64, equalling the course record, one off the Open record.

Woods electrified the gallery at the 17th by holing this chip shot from the hollow for a birdie.

that could save a round, and Woods got the stroke back with a 12-foot birdie putt at the 12th.

Woods made his figures on the next three holes, and then came to the 16th, the last of the par-5 holes. To avoid hitting his ball into the burn that crosses the fairway about 285 yards out, Woods drove with a two iron and hit the ball about 250 yards. Left with about 280 yards to the front of the green, he pulled out his driver, and from bare ground played a marvellous shot that flew toward the green, rolled on, and pulled up about 15 feet from the hole. He holed the putt for an eagle 3.

Six under par, his miracles weren't over yet. Now he approached the 17th, a terrifying par-3 of 223 yards where Nick Price had thrown away the 1982 Open and where Greg Norman made the first of two expensive mistakes that cost him the 1989 championship. Woods' four iron veered left and left him a treacherous chip from a downhill lie in a hollow to a hole cut no more than 18 feet from the green's edge. Woods hooded his wedge and popped the ball into

the face of the upslope. It hit the bank, jumped miles off the ground, rolled toward the cup, took the left-to-right break, and dived into the hole. Another birdie. Seven under now with only the 18th to play.

A drive into the fairway with a seven iron that slipped left into a steep-faced greenside bunker, and then a pitch to 10 feet and still another par saved.

He had played some erratic golf throughout the day, missing fairways and missing greens, and still shot a wonderful score. His drive on the third sailed so far left into the gallery that when he heard a baby crying nearby he asked, "Am I playing that badly?"

Woods had almost finished when first Couples and Parnevik and then Clarke and Leonard began. Couples didn't birdie once in his round of 70, but he holed a full-blooded 168-yard six-iron shot for an eagle 2 on the pitiless 11th and hung within five strokes of Parnevik. Nor could Leonard make headway. He parred the first 10 holes, but he lost strokes on both the 11th and the much easier 12th, where he drove into the rough.

Lee Westwood (210) finished with 67 after playing the second nine in par, three strokes better than in earlier rounds.

Padraig Harrington (213) had his second 69.

Peter Lonard (211) holed out for 2 on the fifth.

The rough at Royal Troon was much different from that at Congressional Country Club, near Washington, where the United States Open had been played a month earlier. Congressional's rough was cultivated. Each blade of grass stood ramrod straight and so densely packed it would twist the club from the player's hands. Troon's rough had been left to grow naturally, festooned with yellow dandelions, bright bluebells, clumps of purple heather, which are the very devil to play from, and stunted gorse, which blooms golden in the springtime. Sometimes the ball lies cleanly in the wispy grass, sometimes the unplayable ball rule is the only escape. Leonard could do no more than pitch back into play and take the bogeys.

Justin had been putting nicely throughout the first two rounds when he shot 69 and 66, but he holed only one putt of any length in the third round, a 25-footer that won him a birdie 2 on the 17th. By then he had been left far behind the leaders, for both Clarke and Parnevik were playing at the top of their games through the first nine.

At first Clarke looked unbeatable. When Parnevik birdied the first two holes, running in putts of 12 and 20 feet, Clarke answered by playing a sand wedge to two feet on the third for one birdie and followed with another on the fourth, where he pitched from a bunker within five feet and holed the putt.

At 11 under par, the Irishman had opened a four-stroke lead over Parnevik, who had made a bogey on the fifth. But Clarke wasn't through. Short of the sixth green with his second shot, he putted across the close-clipped fairway and rolled his ball dead to the hole. Another birdie there and still another on the eighth, where his nine-iron pitch settled 10 feet from the hole. The putt dropped and now Clarke stood 13 under par.

Parnevik, meantime, had recovered from his bogey at the fifth with birdies on the sixth and seventh. His drive on the seventh, which ran much farther than he expected, settled within 50 yards of the green. Like Clarke on the sixth, Parnevik rapped his ball with his putter. It scooted along the ground, climbed the upslope, ran onto the green and pulled up within 15 feet of the cup. He holed it and finished the first nine in 33, three under par.

Still he had lost a stroke to Clarke, who looked nothing at all like quitting. Now, though, they were

Jack Nicklaus (218) went out in 32 but shot 71.

Tom Watson (211) saved par on the sixth.

coming to Parnevik's part of the golf course. He owned the second nine, which had been a mystery to everyone else. In his first two rounds he had shot 34 and 33, three under par, and now he began eating away at Clarke's lead.

He picked up one stroke by birdieing the 10th, where he holed from 15 feet, and another when Clarke hooked his drive into gorse along the left side of the 11th and could do nothing but hack his ball back into play. Clarke's four-stroke lead was down to three now because up ahead Parnevik had dropped a stroke on the 12th, where he missed both the green and a four-foot putt.

Parnevik finished with birdies on the 16th with a pitch to six feet and the 17th with one of the finest iron shots of the week, a three iron that streaked directly at the flagstick and stopped within three feet of the cup.

With a routine par 4 on the 18th, Parnevik had come back in 33 once again and shot 66 for the round. Amazingly, with his second 33 he had played the homeward nine five under par in the first three rounds. Nor had he done badly on the first nine, shooting one 36 and two 33s, six under an easier par.

While Parnevik held onto his game, Clarke lost control of his shots, hitting everything to the right. He made bogeys on both the 11th and 13th holes. He pushed his drive into knotty rough on the 13th, chopped at it with a five iron and cried, "Fore, left!" as the ball flew into even deeper rough near a scoreboard. With no reasonable hope to play a shot from his terrible lie, he took relief and hit a wedge that rolled within six feet of the hole. He holed it, happy for the bogey. Another stroke gone; now he led by two.

He saved himself by holing from eight feet for a par on the 14th, the par-3, but lost both strokes of his lead on the 15th, where he missed another green and a putt of 10 feet that could have saved him. Just then Parnevik birdied the 16th, a swing of two strokes. Now Clarke and Parnevik were tied, although not for long.

Jesper moved one stroke ahead when he birdied the 17th while Clarke could do no better than a

Greg Norman (212) bogeyed two holes coming in.

Curtis Strange (212) was also a television commentator.

par 5 on the 16th, and his lead jumped to two strokes when Clarke bogeyed the 18th.

Darren's last three holes had been adventures. He missed the 16th green with his approach and chipped to five feet to save par, saved another par at the 17th, where he missed another green to the right and holed from about 20 feet, and drove into the right rough again on the 18th and three-putted.

Looking back, Clarke said, "I just seemed to lose the ball right the whole way around the second nine. Missing fairways around that back nine — it's impossible to hit the ball close to the flags, never mind on the green.

"At the same time, I'm only two strokes behind Jesper. If I can get off to a good start tomorrow, maybe I'll play the back nine better than I did today."

Parnevik, meanwhile, looked ahead to the last round as well, but from a different perspective.

Referring to the 1994 Open, where he led playing the last hole, tried a risky pitch and lost the championship to Nick Price, Jesper said, "I have already finished second, so it's not like I don't know what to expect. I've done that. I've finished second, so it doesn't matter to me to finish second again. I'm going out to win."

Bernhard Langer (215) shot a third-round 69.

THIRD ROUND RESULTS

HOLE	1	2	3	4	5	6	7	8	9	10	11	12	13	14	15	16	17	18	
PAR	4	4	4	5	3	5	4	3	4	4	4	4	4	3	4	5	3	4	TOTAL
Jesper Parnevik	3	3	4	5	4	4	3	3	4	3	4	5	4	3	4	4	2	4	66-202
Darren Clarke	4	4	3	4	3	4	2	4	4	5	4	5	3	5	5	5	3	5	71-204
Fred Couples	4	4	4	5	3	5	4	3	4	4	2	4	3	4	5	4	4	70-207
Justin Leonard	4	4	4	5	3	5	4	3	4	4	5	5	3	4	5	2	4		72-207
Stephen Ames	4	3	4	4	3	5	4	3	4	4	4	4	2	3	5	2	4		66-209
Eduardo Romero	4	4	3	5	2	5	3	3	4	4	5	3	3	3	4	5	2	5	67-209
Jim Furyk	5	4	4	4	4	5	4	4	4	3	3	5	3	4	4	2	4		70-209
Tiger Woods	3	3	4	4	4	4	3	3	4	4	5	3	4	3	3	2	4		64-210
Robert Allenby	3	4	4	4	3	5	3	4	4	4	3	4	5	2	4	4	3	3	66-210
Lee Westwood	5	3	4	4	3	4	3	2	4	5	4	5	4	2	4	5	2	4	67-210
Peter Lonard	4	4	4	4	2	5	4	3	4	4	5	4	4	2	4	5	3	4	69-211
Tom Watson	5	4	4	5	3	5	3	4	4	4	4	4	4	3	4	4	2	4	70-211

HOLE SUMMARY

HOLE	PAR	EAGLES	BIRDIES	PARS	BOGEYS	HIGHER	RANK	AVERAGE
1	4	0	15	46	7	2	12	3.94
2	4	0	13	52	4	1	14	3.90
3	4	0	6	58	5	1	11	4.01
4	5	2	40	24	4	0	18	4.43
5	3	0	8	49	13	0	9	3.07
6	5	3	23	38	6	0	16	4.67
7	4	0	23	44	2	1	17	3.73
8	3	0	14	42	11	3	8	3.09
9	4	0	3	61	6	0	10	4.04
OUT	36	5	145	414	58	8		34.88
10	4	0	3	42	22	3	2	4.36
11	4	1	3	37	25	4	1	4.44
12	4	0	7	45	16	2	5	4.19
13	4	0	3	44	22	1	4	4.30
14	3	0	16	44	9	1	13	2.93
15	4	0	3	45	19	3	3	4.33
16	5	1	18	49	2	0	15	4.74
17	3	0	14	35	18	3	6	3.14
18	4	0	8	46	15	1	7	4.13
IN	35	2	75	387	148	18		36.56
TOTAL	71	7	220	801	206	26		71.44

Players Below Par	29
Players At Par	5
Players Above Par	36

WEATHER

Fine, dry and sunny.
Wind 10-15 m.p.h. northwesterly, easing later.

LOW SCORES

Low First Nine	Stuart Appleby	32
	Darren Clarke	32
	Steve Jones	32
	Jack Nicklaus	32
	Lee Westwood	32
	Tiger Woods	32
Low Second Nine	Robert Allenby	32
	Stephen Ames	32
	Jim Furyk	32
	Tiger Woods	32
Low Round	Tiger Woods	64

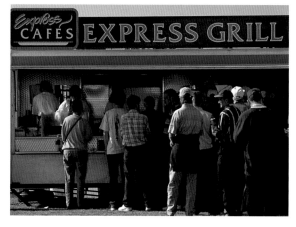

"I probably tried too many high-risk shots in the past," Darren Clarke said. "My aggression usually got me into trouble."

COMMENTARY

DIFFERENT STYLES, SAME GOAL

BY ALISTER NICOL

Two men who would be king dreamed of a coronation at Royal Troon when a dramatic third round was concluded. Sweden's extroverted Jesper Parnevik and Ulster's gentle giant Darren Clarke had emerged as the heirs apparent to Tom Lehman's throne at the end of another day of summer weather transported, it seemed, from the Costa del Sol to Costa Clyde.

Royal Troon was as docile as a drowsy kitten on the third day of the Open Championship and a feline of the man-eating variety gorged himself on the tempting fare presented on a hot day with barely a zephyr to flutter the flags. Tiger Woods shot a course record-equalling 64.

Even those heroics, however, left Woods eight shots behind the 54-hole leader, Parnevik, who carded a 66 of his own. That gap had the Swede in the funny hat and trousers from a bygone fashion era predicting, "Tiger will need to break 60 to win tomorrow."

Golf, as we all know, is an inexact science, with the sport's only certainty its fickle unpredictability. Ask Clarke, the 28-year-old from Dungannon who had led by two strokes after the second round. After nine holes on Saturday he had stretched that advantage to four. Nine holes later, he was trailing by two after a 71.

Darren's opening rounds of 67 and 66 were mirror images of the scores posted by Bobby Clampett in the 1982 Open at Royal Troon, and Clampett, now a television commentator, faded swiftly from the scene.

Clampett followed his stellar rounds with rounds of 77 and 78 to finish four strokes behind winner Tom Watson, who had been seven adrift at the halfway stage. Clarke refused to countenance a similar occurrence, preferring to dwell on the fact that if he were to win the £250,000 first prize on the Sunday he would be the first Irishman since fellow Ulsterman Fred Daly to lift the old claret jug 50 years ago.

Clarke is a big lad with a liking for the odd pint

now and again, while his main protagonist, Parnevik, has a much more exotic taste in beverages. He swills down a dozen spoonfuls of volcanic dust on a monthly basis "to cleanse the intestine of mercury." What, I asked the son of Sweden's most famous show business star, Bo Parnevik, who is a comedian and impersonator, did the concoction taste like?

"Like dirt, what do you think?" Jesper said. "Just like dirt. But it does me good."

Parnevik felt, however, what would do him more good in his quest for Open Championship glory, was the fact that he had "been there" before. That was down the Ayrshire coast at Turnberry in 1994 when he finished runner-up to Nick Price.

"I know what it is like to be in contention in the Open," Parnevik said. "It is something new for Darren. I think the Turnberry experience will work in my favour." It is certainly something he will never be allowed to forget.

A mental aberration saw him fail to read the giant scoreboards round the course that fateful Sunday and he came to the last thinking he needed a birdie to beat the fast-finishing Price, when a par would have seen him in a play-off. He bogeyed the 72nd instead. "I never thought to look at the scoreboard," he later confessed.

Yet thinking is something Florida-based Parnevik does a lot. He employs his own sports psychologist, Olof Skipper, an expert in extra-sensory perception who, from his home in Stockholm, beams advice to Jesper wherever he is in the world. He also has his own philosopher. The duties of Alexander Markus entail keeping Jesper's brain cells active.

It was at the suggestion of Markus that his pupil occasionally wears battery-powered strobe light spectacles to "help synchronise the neutral firings in the brain."

With his weird dress sense and the upturned bill on his cap which, he says, helps him read the line of

"I dress the way I do," Jesper Parnevik said, "because I don't think the game should be taken too seriously."

putts better, even though it was started just to improve his tan, is Jesper Parnevik truly wacky?

"Maybe a little spacey, I guess, my Dad's influence," he said.

Life around the Swede is never dull. Some years ago in a Benson and Hedges International at St Mellion in Cornwall, Jesper was third, then shot an 85 to hurtle down the leaderboard like a downhill skier.

After signing his horrendous card he scattered the ducks in the adjacent pond by throwing himself, fully clothed, into the water. Why? "Because that is what an 85 deserved," responded the dripping, shivering Parnevik.

His credentials for this year's Open were near-flawless. He arrived in Britain with US earnings of close on $800,000 despite being winless. He played well in the Gulfstream Loch Lomond World Invitational the week preceding the Royal Troon spectacular, and indeed claimed to be striking the ball better than ever, although he did not score very well.

"Golf is a very maddening game," Parnevik said after his second-round 66 which bolstered his hopes of going one better than at Turnberry in 1994. "It is probably the most frustrating game of all and one of the reasons I dress the way I do is because I don't think the game should be taken too seriously. But it is tough not to take it seriously because it is such a mind-boggling game. Then if you do take it too seriously, it's going to drive you mad — and that is something a lot of professionals have noticed.

"Then again, you have to take the game with a bit of a laugh most of the time because there are so many things involved which you can't control — like bad bounces, spike marks on greens or whatever. It is definitely a tough game to play for a living."

An opening 70 followed by two 66s were definitely grounds for optimism for the Swede as he turned back the covers of his bed on Saturday night.

Clarke also had reason to be proud of his work over the first three days, despite a slack back nine of 41 in the third round which saw his four-shot edge develop into a two-stroke deficit.

The residents of the wee town of Dungannon were certainly proud. Tipping the scales at 16 stone, Clarke is a broth of a boy. His father, Godfery, was green-keeper at Dungannon Golf Club and that's where his strapping son first struck a golf ball and revealed his potential to be a world-beater. Now a fee-paying member at the much classier Royal Portrush, Darren has never forgotten his roots.

When Dungannon recently needed some re-design work, Darren did it for nothing. And when the town raised £32,000 in a single day for the Marie Curie Cancer Research fund, most of the cash was raised by the sale of material donated by Clarke.

A genial giant off the course, the Irishman will readily admit to being more than a little fiery with clubs in hand. Filled to the brim with natural talent, he has occasionally become too hot-headed for his own good, too aggressive and too ready to hit the self-destruct button when things have not gone the way he wanted.

"I probably tried too many high-risk shots in the past," said the Irish speed-freak who is already on his third Ferrari. "It was my aggression which usually got me into trouble in the past. It is controlled now and I've stopped getting so angry with myself."

He rids himself of much of his frustrations by screaming round Northern Ireland's Kirkiston circuit in racing cars, an indulgence which sometimes horrifies his manager, Andrew "Chubby" Chandler.

Chandler is convinced it is only a matter of time before his client lands a major title. "It's possible Darren saw the winning line before he was ready to win," said Chandler at Troon. "He is beginning to be better able to handle his temperament at exactly the right time. This is only his ninth major, and regardless of what happens in tomorrow's final round, this week will not be a one-off. There are plenty of big ones in Darren."

It is now history that Darren's shanked three-iron tee shot from the second tee onto the Troon beach in the final round effectively killed his hopes. It is also a matter of record that Parnevik's bid for top billing at Sunday's ceremony once again crumbled slowly but so inexorably over the crucial closing holes. For him, the bitter taste of frustrating defeat for a second time must be even worse than the cocktail of water and volcanic dust he downs so regularly.

With his 65, Justin Leonard (272) equalled the record five-stroke comebacks of Jim Barnes and Tommy Armour.

LEONARD EQUALS A RECORD

BY ROBERT SOMMERS

If, after playing the sixth hole at Royal Troon, you walk to the top of the hill behind the green and look southward toward the old town of Prestwick, you can see the holes of the Prestwick Golf Club winding through the rough dunesland. It was over Prestwick's quirky 12-hole course that championship golf as we know it was born. In 1860 Prestwick sent invitations to all clubs to enter two professionals to play for a championship belt of red Morocco leather trimmed with silver.

Only eight men arrived on a chilly October morning and plodded three times around Prestwick's 12 holes. In a classic struggle between two giants of the game, Willie Park, a Musselburgh man, shot 55, three strokes better than Old Tom Morris, who was based in Prestwick then. Both men shot 59 in the second round, and in the third time around, Morris picked up only one stroke. The championship went to Park, 174-176. No one else was close.

The tournament arranged by Prestwick, and played over its grounds for the first 12 years, eventually became known as the Open Championship.

The Open continued to be played periodically at Prestwick when other courses joined the rota. It had been turned into a conventional 18-hole course by the beginning of the century, and the Open into a 72-hole test, but it had been cramped into too small an area to handle galleries safely. Prestwick held its last Open in 1925.

This was the Open Macdonald Smith was supposed to win. A Carnoustie man, Smith won 24 professional tournaments in the United States from 1924 through 1936, but never won a major championship, although he came close. He went into the last round of the 1925 Open with 221, five strokes better than both Archie Compston, an Englishman, and Jim Barnes, another Englishman who had become an American citizen.

With his supporters swarming over the links and urging him on, Smith fell apart. He shot 82 while Barnes swept round in 74, and with 300 beat Compston and Ted Ray by one stroke. Smith dropped to fourth place at 303.

Barnes had made up five strokes. Six years later, in the 1931 Open at Carnoustie, Tommy Armour, an Edinburgh man who had become an American citizen, also came from five strokes behind over the final round for a 296 total to win by one over Jose Jurado of Argentina. Armour shot 71 and Jurado, 77, while Percy Alliss, the father of Peter Alliss, and Gene Sarazen both shot 73 to tie for third place with 298 totals. Armour had 24 US professional victories, the same total as Smith, from 1920 through 1938, but Armour's included the 1927 US Open and 1930 USPGA Championship.

Over the next 65 years no one so far behind after 54 holes had won the Open Championship. Then, within sight of Barnes' great moment, Justin Leonard began the final 18 holes five strokes behind Jesper Parnevik, and with a wonderful round of 65, Leonard caught and passed him and claimed the 126th Open Championship. He shot 272 for the 72 holes, an exceptionally fine score over so difficult a course.

While Leonard was thriving, Parnevik couldn't control his game, missing fairways, greens and critical putts. He shot 73, lost eight strokes to Leonard, and with a 275 total, fell into a tie for second place with Darren Clarke, who had gone into the last round in second place, two strokes behind him. Clarke shot 71.

Jim Furyk of the weird swing shot 70 and placed fourth, with 279, and Padraig Harrington closed with 67 and tied Stephen Ames for fifth place, at 280. Fred Couples, who was expected to challenge Parnevik, could do nothing, shot 74, and fell from a tie for third into a tie for seventh, beside Eduardo Romero and Peter O'Malley.

Leonard played a truly remarkable round. His 65

Darren Clarke (275) was disappointed with his level-par 71 finish, saying, "I expected more of myself."

was the second best round of the week, missing Tiger Woods' 64 by one stroke, and some called it the equal of some of the great closing rounds in recent Opens — Greg Norman's 64 at Sandwich in 1993 when Nick Faldo and Bernhard Langer were shooting 67s behind him, the magnificent 65 by Tom Watson at Turnberry in 1977 that nipped Jack Nicklaus by one stroke, and Seve Ballesteros' 65 at Royal Lytham and St Annes in 1988 in a stroke-for-stroke battle with Nick Price.

Only Leonard among those in position to win had the will, the shots and the control of himself to produce winning golf. Of the last 18 players to tee off, only he shot in the 60s. Those who watched will forever remember the series of putts he holed at the finish. Nor will they forget that he played wonderful approaches that consistently put him in position to birdie. Over the first nine he laid seven pitches within 15 feet of the cup, and only two of those braked more than 10 feet away. From the sixth through the ninth he was awesome. He pitched to four feet on the sixth, to two and a half feet on the seventh, and to

six feet on the ninth. He birdied every one.

He played nearly flawless and nerveless golf, especially on the greens. A sensational putter as an amateur, Leonard holed everything he looked at, particularly at the end when he ran home putts from 15 feet to save par on the 15th, from 15 feet again to birdie the 16th, and from 30 feet on the 17th for his final birdie of the day.

His relentless attacking golf drove Parnevik to commit mistakes he had avoided through the first three rounds. Jesper was shattered by the result. When it ended, he admitted that Leonard's final rush, "took the wind out of my sails."

Two strokes ahead with seven to play, Parnevik finished weakly, missing a precious birdie opening on the 16th, and then bogeying both the 17th and 18th, and falling into a tie with Clarke.

Only one player scored within a stroke of Leonard in the final round. Tom Lehman closed the disappointing defence of his 1996 Open Championship with 66, which, aside from soothing his spirits, lifted him into a tie for 24th place, at 284, in an eight-man

"This one hurt a lot more than Turnberry (in 1994)," said Jesper Parnevik (275) of his second runner-up showing.

A pair of 70s on the weekend lifted Jim Furyk (279) to fourth place, seven strokes off the winning score.

Padraig Harrington (280) started with 75, then posted three scores in the 60s to tie for fifth place.

group including Colin Montgomerie, Phil Mickelson, Ian Woosnam and Tiger Woods, who slipped backwards with 74.

Once again the galleries showed how much they like Lehman. As he walked into the great amphitheatre of the 18th, with crowded grandstands rising both left and right of him, the crowds cheered and applauded warmly, almost as if he had won. He had gone out in mid-morning with the goal of finishing under par for the championship, but he would have had to shoot 65 to do it. Instead, he settled for level par. This was his reward. He loved it.

"The reception coming up the 18th was unbelievable," he said. "It makes me feel I was appreciated and that the fans like me. I like that. I look forward to the day when I get that reception by winning again. Everyone has been so gracious and sincerely warm. I walked into a restaurant last night and everyone clapped. You don't get that in the States."

No one, though, was cheered more enthusiastically than Nicklaus. The galleries greeted him on every green. They had something to cheer about when he played the first nine in 35, a stroke under par, but he came back in 40, shot 293, and tied for 60th place with Barclay Howard, the low amateur. His fans didn't care what he shot, though; they savoured sim-

Eduardo Romero (281) tied for seventh place.

A level-par 71 enabled Stephen Ames (280) to stroll to a share of fifth place.

Peter O'Malley (281) finished with 68.

Fred Couples (281) had 74, his worst score.

ply the sight of him in the Open Championship once again.

Troon was much the same as it had been the previous two days, although dull grey clouds blocked out the sun through much of the day and the wind picked up just a little. It was warm and pleasant, the sun broke through in the afternoon, and it was a delightful day for golf.

Playing under such mild conditions, 26 men broke par 71 and 11 others matched it. Some scores were worth mentioning. Ernie Els played his third consecutive 69, but he had been ruined by his opening 75. Frank Nobilo shot a second consecutive 68. Davis Love III, Brad Faxon and Jose Maria Olazabal shot 67s, and Tom Watson closed with 71 and tied for 10th place with nine others, among them Els, Love, Tom Kite and Mark Calcavecchia.

Some of the early starters showed Troon would give in to good golf. Corey Pavin, the second man off the tee, shot 68, the same score as Mark O'Meara and American journeyman John Kernohan. Both

Mark McNulty and Andrew Magee shot 69s, and Faxon began his round of 67 more than half an hour before noon.

Tiger Woods started in the fourth-from-last group, paired with Furyk. After his blistering 64 of Saturday, Tiger trailed Parnevik by eight strokes and Clarke by six. Another round in the middle 60s and who knows what might happen. The early holes, so vulnerable to attack, might tell, for one with Woods' length could nearly drive the greens, certainly leaving no more than a sand wedge for the approach.

From the first it looked as if this wouldn't be Tiger's day. He bunkered his approach to the first and scraped out a par, hit his second shot to the second more than 50 feet from the hole and parred again.

The third offered a further clue. His pitch settled eight feet from the cup, but the birdie putt slipped past the hole. Three straight pars on holes where you must make a birdie or two.

He did indeed birdie both the fourth and fifth, and

Shigeki Maruyama (282) recorded his second 69.

once again his putting stroke let him down. He missed from eight feet again on the sixth, from three feet on the seventh, and then his Open ended on the eighth, the Postage Stamp hole. His nine-iron tee shot buried itself in a deep greenside bunker on the right, and a timid recovery shot rolled back down the hillside to his feet. He came out 25 feet from the cup with his third shot, rammed his first putt four feet past the hole, and missed coming back. He made 6, losing three strokes to par on one hole. That finished him. He played listless golf the rest of the way.

While Woods struggled, Parnevik, Clarke and Leonard moved ahead. Parnevik arrived wearing a white cap with its peak turned up, of course, white shirt, white shoes and skimpy purple trousers that turned many a head. He began slowly, parring the first two holes. Still 11 under par, he birdied the third to go to 12 under, but then committed the sin of bogeying a par-5 hole.

After a nice drive on the sixth, he hit his second about as well as he could hit a ball, but he had started it too far right. It flew into a fairway bunker, leaving no opening to the green. He pitched out as best he could, and remembering how wonderfully he had played his putter from the seventh fairway the previous day, he tried it again. He played it not nearly as well, took two putts from more than 20 feet, and made 6. He had a great break at the seventh when his approach, certain to run over the green, took one bounce, tangled itself in the flag and nearly dropped into the hole, and he birdied, his third 3 on the seventh in three days. Back to 12 under par. Two more pars and he made the turn for home in 35.

Playing along with Parnevik, Clarke had about given up hope. He had birdied the first, but then hit what he called the worst shank of his career. The ball squirted off toward the beach and out of bounds. He made 6 with a nice recovery from a bunker and never again threatened to win.

Leonard, meanwhile, had been playing up ahead and making one birdie after another. Six under at the start, he birdied the second, third and fourth holes, lost a stroke at the fifth, where he three-putted, missing his second from no more than four feet, then played the first in a series of marvellous pitches.

From bare ground short of the sixth green he played a sand wedge to four feet; his wedge to the seventh looked as if it might jump into the hole but stopped about two feet away; his 25-foot putt on the eighth hung over the lip of the cup but didn't fall, and his eight iron to the ninth came down right of the green, but took the roll of the ground and came to rest perhaps six feet away. He birdied them all. In an instruction-book first nine, he had hit every green, birdied six holes, and with his lone bogey, shot 31. From six under par at the start, he had gone to 11 under par and climbed within one stroke of Parnevik.

Leonard's was a serious threat because Parnevik had been playing loose golf, pulling his shots throughout the day and saving himself consistently with deft work around the greens. Even though he hit only four greens on the first nine, he had gone out in 35, one under par, mainly because he had putted only 11 times. His short game had been deadly.

Both Parnevik and Leonard bogeyed the 10th, and Parnevik looked as if he had saved the championship on the 11th, Troon's most severe hole. Once again his drive drifted left into light rough, and from there

Retief Goosen (282) shot 68 to finish well.

Frank Nobilo (282) closed with two 68s.

he played a terrific iron that hit the green and rolled hole-high about 18 or 20 feet left of the hole. The putt dropped. On a hole where everyone else would have been satisfied to par, Parnevik had birdied it twice. Twelve under par again, he led Leonard by two strokes with the hardest part of the course coming up.

Leonard's putting had been hard to believe, and now he seemed to hole everything. After bogeying the 10th, where his pitch from the left rough ran off the back of the green, he took three shots to reach the 11th but holed from 10 feet, missed the 12th green from the rough but chipped to one foot and saved par, and made routine pars on the 13th and 14th.

Parnevik lost one stroke of his lead when he pushed his approach to the 13th. The ball hit a high dune, bounced toward the green, but caught a downslope and rolled down the hill away from the green. His pitch settled 10 feet or more from the hole, and his putt grazed the cup but missed. Back to 11 under par.

The 15th probably turned the Open around.

Leonard pushed his drive into the wispy rough, couldn't reach the green, and played an indifferent pitch to 15 feet. He had to hole this putt; he trailed Parnevik by one stroke and the holes were running out. If he lost a stroke here he might not have enough holes to make it up. Taking his time finding the line, Leonard rolled the ball right into the cup. Still 10 under.

Now began the string of holes that won the Open for Leonard. Two shots placed him short of the 16th green, and he played another indifferent pitch that pulled up 15 feet short of the hole again. Never mind; he had made a putt of the same length on the 15th, and now he made another. When it dropped he had caught Parnevik playing one hole behind him.

Parnevik had seen Leonard's birdie on the 16th and now he heard another birdie on the 17th. A three-iron shot had rolled onto the green and Leonard holed from 30 feet. The roar of the crowd told Parnevik all he needed to know.

Leonard had gone ahead at 12 under par, but back at the 16th, Parnevik had a short putt for a birdie of his own. A marvellous pitch to three feet assured him

A 15-foot putt on the 15th provided Leonard with a crucial par, one of six putts of 10 feet or more.

Couples congratulated the new champion.

of the birdie he needed, but his ball drifted right and the putt ran over the right edge of the cup. He made his par, but that wasn't good enough.

Up ahead on the 18th tee, Leonard, knowing he had to avoid the fairway bunkers, drove with his three wood. Championships are often decided by narrow margins. Parnevik's putt, for example, could have fallen but it didn't, and Leonard's drive could have run into a bunker, but it didn't either. It missed rolling into the first fairway bunker on the left by less than a foot. From there he played a safe shot onto the green and got down in two putts for the par.

By the time Leonard struck his first putt, it was all over, for Parnevik had pulled another shot left and bogeyed the 17th. When he bogeyed the 18th as well, and Clarke birdied, he finished three strokes out of first place.

His losing had been a serious blow to his morale. This was the second Open he might have won and yet had it taken from him when he stumbled over the late holes. He simply had not been capable of playing his best golf on the important occasions.

Leonard, on the other hand, had played his best golf when he needed it most, and he gave the rest of the field a post-graduate course in pressure putting.

He is 25 years of age, the third successive American to win the Open, the fifth successive American to have won at Troon, and the third man in his 20s to win the major championships of 1997. Woods, 21, won the Masters, and Ernie Els, 27, won the United States Open.

Before he turned to professional golf, in 1994, Leonard had been a first-class amateur. He won the 1992 United States Amateur and two years later the NCAA, the American collegiate championship, tying the record Phil Mickelson had set in 1992. Because of an unfortunate act of timing, he wasn't given much credit for his amateur record because he fit between Mickelson and Tiger Woods.

More compact than either of them, Leonard stands 5 feet, 9 inches, and weighs 11½ stone, about the same as Ben Hogan in his later years. Like Hogan, he is from Texas; but Leonard lives in Dallas, Hogan lived in Fort Worth, not far away. While his swing is flat, like Hogan's, he doesn't have that high finish so typical of Ben; his finish looks even flatter than his backswing. Nor does he have Hogan's long extension through the ball.

Unlike Hogan, though, Leonard comes from a fairly well-to-do family, and went to the University of Texas. He dresses neatly and conservatively, and always makes a nice appearance. Furthermore, he loves playing in the Open, and has said he would like to play sometime wearing a collar and tie.

He had had to go through qualifying in his first two Opens, in 1993 and 1995, and he said at Troon that whether he's exempt or not, "I'm going to come over and try to qualify."

That won't be necessary; as the 1997 champion, he's eligible through 2037, the year he reaches 65 years of age.

Leonard acknowledged the cheers from the grandstands after holing out for his 65 and eventual three-stroke victory.

FOURTH ROUND RESULTS

HOLE	1	2	3	4	5	6	7	8	9	10	11	12	13	14	15	16	17	18	TOTAL
PAR	4	4	4	5	3	5	4	3	4	4	4	4	4	3	4	5	3	4	TOTAL
Justin Leonard	4	3	3	4	4	4	3	3	3	5	4	4	4	3	4	4	2	4	65-272
Darren Clarke	3	6	4	5	3	4	4	3	5	4	4	4	4	3	5	4	3	3	71-275
Jesper Parnevik	4	4	3	5	3	6	3	3	4	5	3	4	5	3	4	5	4	5	73-275
Jim Furyk	4	4	4	5	3	5	4	4	4	4	4	4	4	3	4	4	3	4	70-279
Padraig Harrington	3	4	3	4	3	4	3	4	4	4	4	3	5	3	5	3	4	4	67-280
Stephen Ames	5	6	4	5	3	4	4	3	4	3	4	4	3	3	4	5	3	4	71-280
Peter O'Malley	4	4	3	3	3	4	3	3	4	4	4	4	5	3	4	5	4	4	68-281
Eduardo Romero	4	4	4	5	3	5	3	4	4	4	5	4	3	3	4	5	4	4	72-281
Fred Couples	3	5	4	5	4	4	4	3	4	4	4	5	4	4	5	5	3	4	74-281

HOLE SUMMARY

HOLE	PAR	EAGLES	BIRDIES	PARS	BOGEYS	HIGHER	RANK	AVERAGE
1	4	0	15	45	8	2	13	3.96
2	4	0	8	48	11	3	7	4.13
3	4	0	12	54	4	0	15	3.89
4	5	7	38	23	2	0	18	4.29
5	3	0	5	49	16	0	5	3.16
6	5	0	29	31	9	1	16	4.74
7	4	0	18	42	9	1	14	3.90
8	3	0	14	35	15	6	3	3.21
9	4	0	11	49	10	0	12	3.99
OUT	36	7	150	376	84	13		35.27
10	4	0	8	48	14	0	9	4.09
11	4	0	3	44	14	9	1	4.47
12	4	0	7	50	11	2	8	4.11
13	4	0	6	44	19	1	6	4.21
14	3	0	9	48	13	0	11	3.06
15	4	0	3	44	21	2	2	4.31
16	5	1	24	41	4	0	17	4.69
17	3	0	9	39	21	1	4	3.20
18	4	0	9	48	12	1	9	4.09
IN	35	1	78	406	129	16		36.23
TOTAL	71	8	228	782	213	29		71.50

Players Below Par	26
Players At Par	11
Players Above Par	33

WEATHER

Fine and dry.
Wind light and variable.

LOW SCORES

Low First Nine	Justin Leonard	31
	Peter O'Malley	31
Low Second Nine	Stephen Ames	33
	Brad Faxon	33
	Tom Lehman	33
	Davis Love III	33
	Colin Montgomerie	33
	Frank Nobilo	33
	David A. Russell	33
Low Round	Justin Leonard	65

CHAMPIONSHIP HOLE SUMMARY

HOLE	PAR	YARDS	EAGLES	BIRDIES	PARS	BOGEYS	HIGHER	RANK	AVERAGE
1	4	364	1	93	303	44	7	16	3.92
2	4	391	0	62	329	49	8	13	4.01
3	4	379	0	60	320	65	3	12	4.02
4	5	557	20	227	175	25	1	18	4.46
5	3	210	1	39	312	93	3	9	3.13
6	5	577	9	174	220	40	5	17	4.68
7	4	402	0	87	300	52	9	14	3.96
8	3	126	1	80	252	87	28	7	3.17
9	4	423	0	57	311	74	6	11	4.07
OUT	36	3429	32	879	2522	529	70		35.42
10	4	438	0	20	216	177	35	2	4.52
11	4	463	1	17	212	158	60	1	4.65
12	4	431	0	36	295	106	11	8	4.21
13	4	465	0	27	235	161	25	5	4.42
14	3	179	1	54	290	94	9	9	3.13
15	4	457	0	17	246	164	21	4	4.43
16	5	542	2	99	291	48	8	15	4.92
17	3	223	0	36	249	140	23	3	3.35
18	4	452	0	34	248	133	33	6	4.38
IN	35	3650	4	340	2282	1181	225		38.01
TOTAL	71	7079	36	1219	4804	1710	295		73.43

	FIRST ROUND	SECOND ROUND	THIRD ROUND	FOURTH ROUND	TOTAL
Players Below Par	10	45	29	26	110
Players At Par	6	15	5	11	37
Players Above Par	140	92	36	33	301

RELATIVE DIFFICULTY OF HOLES

HOLE	PAR	YARDS	FIRST ROUND	SECOND ROUND	THIRD ROUND	FOURTH ROUND	OVERALL RANK
1	4	364	16	16	12	13	16
2	4	391	15	13	14	7	13
3	4	379	12	14	11	15	12
4	5	557	18	18	18	18	18
5	3	210	10	8	9	5	9
6	5	577	17	17	16	16	17
7	4	402	13	11	17	14	14
8	3	126	7	10	8	3	7
9	4	423	11	11	10	12	11
10	4	438	3	2	2	9	2
11	4	463	1	1	1	1	1
12	4	431	8	9	5	8	8
13	4	465	2	6	4	6	5
14	3	179	9	6	13	11	9
15	4	457	6	4	3	2	4
16	5	542	13	15	15	17	15
17	3	223	4	3	6	4	3
18	4	452	5	5	7	9	6

"A wonderful day, a wonderful week," Justin Leonard said. "To make those three putts in a row was so exciting."

GRASPING THE HALF CHANCE

BY JOHN HOPKINS

Golfers become champions because they step forward and grasp a half chance of victory when it is offered to them. This is what Justin Leonard did just after teatime on a sunlit afternoon. Behind him, Jesper Parnevik, the leader after 54 holes, was wobbling dangerously, while Darren Clarke, a beefy, engaging Northern Irishman, who had been two strokes behind Parnevik, had faded, too.

Leonard, meanwhile, had scored brilliantly all afternoon. He had closed in on Parnevik from five strokes behind at the start of the day, and as he approached the closing holes of Royal Troon he resembled a 1,500-metres runner coming off the last bend who thinks to himself, "Come on, one last push. I can win this now."

Champions do not always do this the first time it is offered to them. Tom Watson, Severiano Ballesteros and Nick Faldo did not. Nor did Ben Hogan, Arnold Palmer and Greg Norman. But Leonard did. The half chance that was offered to him at Royal Troon was the first in a major championship for the 25-year-old Texan who had only turned professional three years earlier.

Leonard's 65, underpinned by a dazzling display of putting during which he took only 25 putts, was a score that suggested that he went out and grabbed the old claret jug as champions are supposed to do. Many of his rivals had little or no success at this. In the last round Parnevik, Clarke, Watson, Norman, Fred Couples, Tiger Woods and Curtis Strange all either exceeded or equalled their previous worst score in the championship.

There were several moments in the final round when Leonard looked the part of the champion. The first came when he holed a putt of 10 feet to save his par on the 11th. On the 15th it was another putt to save par that helped him to apply more pressure that was ultimately to cause Parnevik to buckle. This one was 15 feet. On the 16th he holed another putt of 15 feet. Then came the final blow, the one that really finished off Parnevik. On the 17th, he hit a three iron to the back of the green and then, 30 feet from the flag, holed the putt.

"I had a real good look at that putt and I saw a spot just outside the right edge of that hole," Leonard recalled. "I don't have any idea if that's where I actually hit the ball, but that's where I was trying to hit it. As soon as it went in, everyone behind me went nuts." Perhaps some of those who went nuts were the staff of the Marine Highland Hotel, where Leonard had been staying in a tiny room all week, who may have sneaked more than an occasional look out of the windows of the hotel to see what was unfolding beneath.

Leonard has been booted and spurred for greatness in golf almost since he took it up as an eight-year-old. That was when his parents started taking him to Royal Oaks, a country club in Dallas, Texas, where the pro was Randy Smith. Leonard was short and skinny in those far-off days and the clubs he used were hand-me-downs from his grandmother which had been cut down. That summer the family went on holiday to Florida. While his peers dug moats with their buckets and spades, Leonard designed a par-5 hole with lots of water on it.

The young Leonard was obsessed by golf. When he had to draw, Leonard drew golf courses. When he had to write essays, Leonard wrote about Jack Nicklaus, Arnold Palmer and Gary Player. When he was ill at home, Leonard chipped golf balls around the inside of his parents' house. "Up the stairs, around the dining room table and over the dog," is how he once described it.

In 1986, when he was 13, Leonard won the Oklahoma Junior Classic. "From then on he just wanted more and more," Smith remembered. "I was giving five lessons a week and two of them were to him. I was busy merchandising, but he brought me back to my mission fast, because you don't often run into a kid like this. A blind man couldn't have screwed him up."

Because Leonard was small, he became accustomed to being outdriven in much the same way as Corey Pavin was. Like Pavin and many other less powerful players, Leonard coped by being a stroke-maker. He concentrated on learning how to manoeuvre the ball and he improved his short game.

He was the US Amateur champion in 1992, competed in the 1993 Walker Cup, and won the 1994 NCAA championship. He missed the cut in the 1993 Open, but came 68th in the US Open. The next year was better — and the year after that was better still. That is a striking aspect of Leonard's career. If it were a graph, it would go steadily upwards. In 1995 he won half a million pounds in prize money, a figure that improved to £650,000 in 1996, the year he played in the Presidents Cup.

He had all the makings of a star and Tom Kite, who had watched Leonard closely — as well as given him dinner in the Kite household when he was younger — was saying no more than was obvious when he said, "I have never seen a player at his age so polished. He is going to win big and he is going to win often. It is only a question of time." Since turning pro Leonard has won nearly £2 million.

Neatness, organisation, a sense of purpose, discipline — these were all Leonard's trademarks and remain so today. He was purposeful in his academic studies at the University of Texas, where Kite and Ben Crenshaw had attended before him, spending most Friday and Saturday evenings studying so that he was able to play golf during the day.

The story is told of how Leonard put in an hour's practice on the eve of a recent Tucson Open. The weather was bleak in Texas, and snow and ice lay on the ground. Leonard drove his Land Rover out to a quiet spot on the practice ground where it would protect him from the wind and cleared the snow. He hit balls for an hour. The next day the weather was even worse, so Leonard limited his practice to 45 minutes.

Big is not a word that is applied to Leonard very often. He is 5 feet, 9 inches, weighs 11½ stone, and

until he changed recently from a persimmon-headed driver to a driver with a titanium head and a graphite shaft with a 45-inch shaft, he was one of the shortest hitters on the USPGA Tour. Significantly, though, Ben Hogan was about the same height and weight and had the same flat swing as Leonard. What is the name Leonard has on the cap he always wears? Hogan.

Some golfers may wear their facial expressions on their sleeves; Leonard hides his beneath that black cap, just as Hogan was rarely seen on a golf course without a white cap. Leonard's swing, like Hogan's, is that of a man who grew up in the wind of Texas. It is flat at the top of the backswing, even flatter at the finish.

With what club did Leonard conclude his warm-up before the fourth round? He chose a one iron, sat the ball on a hillside lie, and after a couple of unsatisfactory strokes, hit eight in a row that ended exactly where he wanted them. Such mastery with the most difficult club in the bag would have impressed Hogan, who, it is said, retired because he could no longer hit one irons from tight fairway lies.

Leonard won twice in four weeks and made sure of his Ryder Cup place where he would be an asset to the US team because of his experience, his putting and his resolute temperament. Leonard became the fifth American to win at Troon, following in the footsteps of Arnold Palmer in 1962, Tom Weiskopf in 1973, Tom Watson in 1982 and Mark Calcavecchia in 1989. He also became the third consecutive American to win the Open.

Leonard joins the gilded youths of American golf who are talented and thrusting their way to the forefront of the game at the expense of Faldo, Norman, Lehman and the like. The emergence of Tiger Woods, the 21-year-old Masters champion, has given the game in the US an unrivalled boost; and the arrival of Leonard, barely four years older than Woods, means that in the past three months the US has produced two new winners of major championships who are not yet 26. Woods is the cornerstone of this group, which also includes Mickelson, 27. With victory in the US Open by Ernie Els, 27, Leonard's success meant that all three major champi-

Caddie Bob Riefke (in red bib) said of Leonard, "I had to keep him calm and tell him 'just let it happen.'"

onships so far this year had been won by men in their 20s.

Leonard is also manically tidy and eerily composed. His victory speech at Troon was prepared well in advance and he carried it in his back pocket. It was right out of a text book, *How to Win Friends and Influence People.* "I'd like to thank Ian Valentine, the club captain; Mr Bonallack, Secretary of the R and A, and the green-keeper for his good work," Leonard began. He did not forget Parnevik and Clarke and even Barclay Howard, the Scottish amateur, who won the silver medal for being the leading amateur. That went down a treat with the crowd.

He looks like the sort of young man mothers want their daughters to bring home. Clean-cut and good-looking, he models clothes for Ralph Lauren. He wears tasselled loafers and sunglasses. At his flat in Dallas, which he shares with his sister, there is a pile of thank-you notes on the kitchen table waiting to be posted. When Kelly, his sister, moved into the flat, Justin made a rule: Beds have to be made each morning. "He makes lists of lists," his sister said, clearly speaking in the few rare moments when she wasn't having to keep the flat clean for her tidy brother. "Justin is the most organized person in the world," Brad Faxon, the US Ryder Cup player, says. "He

probably vacuums in a straight line."

Would Leonard have won at Troon but for the baptism of fire he went through in the Phoenix Open in January 1996 when he was beaten in a play-off by Mickelson? Phoenix attracts some of the largest crowds on the USPGA Tour and almost all of them were supporting Mickelson, the local boy. "Hit in a bunker," they yelled at Leonard. "Miss it," they shouted as he lined up a putt. Mickelson won, but Leonard, demonstrating his maturity and a clear-headed attitude, turned it all to his advantage. Instead of being intimidated by it, he described it as his best learning experience since turning pro.

"I didn't come away with nothing," Leonard said later. "I became stronger mentally from losing in that type of situation. I learned that I have what it takes to win and that I enjoy the pressure. Playing that round was like looking at myself in a microscope. What I saw increased my confidence."

That was why he went on to win the Buick Open in 1996 and the Kemper Open in 1997. He was not afraid any more. He knew how to play the game at the highest level. He was fulfilling what Kite had forecast about him. In other words, he was ready, and that was why, when the half chance was offered to him at Troon, he took it, just as champions do.

Seve Ballesteros (1979, 1984, 1988)

Mark Calcavecchia (1989)

Nick Faldo (1987, 1990, 1992)

Tom Watson (1975, 1977, 1980, 1982, 1983)

Tom Lehman (1996)

OPEN CHAMPIONSHIP

YEAR	CHAMPION	SCORE	MARGIN	RUNNERS-UP	VENUE
1860	Willie Park	174	2	Tom Morris Snr	Prestwick
1861	Tom Morris Snr	163	4	Willie Park	Prestwick
1862	Tom Morris Snr	163	13	Willie Park	Prestwick
1863	Willie Park	168	2	Tom Morris Snr	Prestwick
1864	Tom Morris Snr	167	2	Andrew Strath	Prestwick
1865	Andrew Strath	162	2	Willie Park	Prestwick
1866	Willie Park	169	2	David Park	Prestwick
1867	Tom Morris Snr	170	2	Willie Park	Prestwick
1868	Tom Morris Jnr	157	2	Robert Andrew	Prestwick
1869	Tom Morris Jnr	154	3	Tom Morris Snr	Prestwick
1870	Tom Morris Jnr	149	12	Bob Kirk, David Strath	Prestwick
1871	*No Competition*				
1872	Tom Morris Jnr	166	3	David Strath	Prestwick
1873	Tom Kidd	179	1	Jamie Anderson	St Andrews
1874	Mungo Park	159	2	Tom Morris Jnr	Musselburgh
1875	Willie Park	166	2	Bob Martin	Prestwick
1876	Bob Martin	176	—	David Strath	St Andrews
				(Martin was awarded the title when Strath refused to play-off)	
1877	Jamie Anderson	160	2	Bob Pringle	Musselburgh
1878	Jamie Anderson	157	2	Bob Kirk	Prestwick
1879	Jamie Anderson	169	3	James Allan, Andrew Kirkaldy	St Andrews
1880	Bob Ferguson	162	5	Peter Paxton	Musselburgh
1881	Bob Ferguson	170	3	Jamie Anderson	Prestwick
1882	Bob Ferguson	171	3	Willie Fernie	St Andrews
1883	Willie Fernie	159	Play-off	Bob Ferguson	Musselburgh
				(Fernie won play-off 158 to 159)	
1884	Jack Simpson	160	4	David Rollan, Willie Fernie	Prestwick
1885	Bob Martin	171	1	Archie Simpson	St Andrews
1886	David Brown	157	2	Willie Campbell	Musselburgh
1887	Willie Park Jnr	161	1	Bob Martin	Prestwick
1888	Jack Burns	171	1	David Anderson Jnr, Ben Sayers	St Andrews
1889	Willie Park Jnr	155	Play-off	Andrew Kirkaldy	Musselburgh
				(Park won play-off 158 to 163)	
1890	*John Ball	164	3	Willie Fernie, Archie Simpson	Prestwick
1891	Hugh Kirkaldy	166	2	Willie Fernie, Andrew Kirkaldy	St Andrews
(From 1892 the competition was extended to 72 holes)					
1892	*Harold Hilton	305	3	*John Ball Jnr, James Kirkaldy, Sandy Herd	Muirfield
1893	Willie Auchterlonie	322	2	*Johnny Laidlay	Prestwick

YEAR	CHAMPION	SCORE	MARGIN	RUNNERS-UP	VENUE
1894	J.H. Taylor	326	5	Douglas Rolland	Sandwich
1895	J.H. Taylor	322	4	Sandy Herd	St Andrews
1896	Harry Vardon	316	Play-off	J.H. Taylor	Muirfield
				(Vardon won play-off 157 to 161)	
1897	*Harold H. Hilton	314	1	James Braid	Hoylake
1898	Harry Vardon	307	1	Willie Park	Prestwick
1899	Harry Vardon	310	5	Jack White	Sandwich
1900	J.H. Taylor	309	8	Harry Vardon	St Andrews
1901	James Braid	309	3	Harry Vardon	Muirfield
1902	Sandy Herd	307	1	Harry Vardon, James Braid	Hoylake
1903	Harry Vardon	300	6	Tom Vardon	Prestwick
1904	Jack White	296	1	James Braid, J.H. Taylor	Sandwich
1905	James Braid	318	5	J.H. Taylor, R. Jones	St Andrews
1906	James Braid	300	4	J.H. Taylor	Muirfield
1907	Arnaud Massy	312	2	J.H. Taylor	Hoylake
1908	James Braid	291	8	Tom Ball	Prestwick
1909	J.H. Taylor	295	4	James Braid	Deal
1910	James Braid	299	4	Sandy Herd	St Andrews
1911	Harry Vardon	303	Play-off	Arnaud Massy	Sandwich
				(Play-off; Massy conceded at the 35th hole)	
1912	Ted Ray	295	4	Harry Vardon	Muirfield
1913	J.H. Taylor	304	8	Ted Ray	Hoylake
1914	Harry Vardon	306	3	J.H. Taylor	Prestwick
1915-1919 No Championship					
1920	George Duncan	303	2	Sandy Herd	Deal
1921	Jock Hutchison	296	Play-off	*Roger Wethered	St Andrews
				(Hutchison won play-off 150 to 159)	
1922	Walter Hagen	300	1	George Duncan, Jim Barnes	Sandwich
1923	Arthur G. Havers	295	1	Walter Hagen	Troon
1924	Walter Hagen	301	1	Ernest Whitcombe	Hoylake
1925	Jim Barnes	300	1	Archie Compston, Ted Ray	Prestwick
1926	*Robert T. Jones Jnr	291	2	Al Watrous	Royal Lytham
1927	*Robert T. Jones Jnr	285	6	Aubrey Boomer, Fred Robson	St Andrews
1928	Walter Hagen	292	2	Gene Sarazen	Sandwich
1929	Walter Hagen	292	6	John Farrell	Muirfield
1930	*Robert T. Jones Jnr	291	2	Leo Diegel, Macdonald Smith	Hoylake
1931	Tommy Armour	296	1	Jose Jurado	Carnoustie
1932	Gene Sarazen	283	5	Macdonald Smith	Prince's
1933	Densmore Shute	292	Play-off	Craig Wood	St Andrews
				(Shute won play-off 149 to 154)	
1934	Henry Cotton	283	5	Sid Brews	Sandwich
1935	Alf Perry	283	4	Alf Padgham	Muirfield
1936	Alf Padgham	287	1	Jimmy Adams	Hoylake
1937	Henry Cotton	290	2	Reg Whitcombe	Carnoustie
1938	Reg Whitcombe	295	2	Jimmy Adams	Sandwich
1939	Richard Burton	290	2	Johnny Bulla	St Andrews
1940-1945 No Championship					
1946	Sam Snead	290	4	Bobby Locke, Johnny Bulla	St Andrews
1947	Fred Daly	293	1	Reg Horne, *Frank Stranahan	Hoylake
1948	Henry Cotton	284	5	Fred Daly	Muirfield
1949	Bobby Locke	283	Play-off	Harry Bradshaw	Sandwich
				(Locke won play-off 135 to 147)	
1950	Bobby Locke	279	2	Roberto de Vicenzo	Troon
1951	Max Faulkner	285	2	Tony Cerda	Royal Portrush
1952	Bobby Locke	287	1	Peter Thomson	Royal Lytham

YEAR	CHAMPION	SCORE	MARGIN	RUNNERS-UP	VENUE
1953	Ben Hogan	282	4	*Frank Stranahan, Dai Rees, Peter Thomson, Tony Cerda	Carnoustie
1954	Peter Thomson	283	1	Sid Scott, Dai Rees, Bobby Locke	Royal Birkdale
1955	Peter Thomson	281	2	Johnny Fallon	St Andrews
1956	Peter Thomson	286	3	Flory van Donck	Hoylake
1957	Bobby Locke	279	3	Peter Thomson	St Andrews
1958	Peter Thomson	278	Play-off	David Thomas (Thomson won play-off 139 to 143)	Royal Lytham
1959	Gary Player	284	2	Flory van Donck, Fred Bullock	Muirfield
1960	Kel Nagle	278	1	Arnold Palmer	St Andrews
1961	Arnold Palmer	284	1	Dai Rees	Royal Birkdale
1962	Arnold Palmer	276	6	Kel Nagle	Troon
1963	Bob Charles	277	Play-off	Phil Rodgers (Charles won play-off 140 to 148)	Royal Lytham
1964	Tony Lema	279	5	Jack Nicklaus	St Andrews
1965	Peter Thomson	285	2	Christy O'Connor, Brian Huggett	Royal Birkdale
1966	Jack Nicklaus	282	1	David Thomas, Doug Sanders	Muirfield
1967	Roberto de Vicenzo	278	2	Jack Nicklaus	Hoylake
1968	Gary Player	289	2	Jack Nicklaus, Bob Charles	Carnoustie
1969	Tony Jacklin	280	2	Bob Charles	Royal Lytham
1970	Jack Nicklaus	283	Play-off	Doug Sanders (Nicklaus won play-off 72 to 73)	St Andrews
1971	Lee Trevino	278	1	Lu Liang Huan	Royal Birkdale
1972	Lee Trevino	278	1	Jack Nicklaus	Muirfield
1973	Tom Weiskopf	276	3	Neil Coles, Johnny Miller	Troon
1974	Gary Player	282	4	Peter Oosterhuis	Royal Lytham
1975	Tom Watson	279	Play-off	Jack Newton (Watson won play-off 71 to 72)	Carnoustie
1976	Johnny Miller	279	6	Jack Nicklaus, Severiano Ballesteros	Royal Birkdale
1977	Tom Watson	268	1	Jack Nicklaus	Turnberry
1978	Jack Nicklaus	281	2	Simon Owen, Ben Crenshaw, Raymond Floyd, Tom Kite	St Andrews
1979	Severiano Ballesteros	283	3	Jack Nicklaus, Ben Crenshaw	Royal Lytham
1980	Tom Watson	271	4	Lee Trevino	Muirfield
1981	Bill Rogers	276	4	Bernhard Langer	Sandwich
1982	Tom Watson	284	1	Peter Oosterhuis, Nick Price	Troon
1983	Tom Watson	275	1	Hale Irwin, Andy Bean	Royal Birkdale
1984	Severiano Ballesteros	276	2	Bernhard Langer, Tom Watson	St Andrews
1985	Sandy Lyle	282	1	Payne Stewart	Sandwich
1986	Greg Norman	280	5	Gordon J. Brand	Turnberry
1987	Nick Faldo	279	1	Rodger Davis, Paul Azinger	Muirfield
1988	Severiano Ballesteros	273	2	Nick Price	Royal Lytham
1989	Mark Calcavecchia	275	Play-off	Greg Norman, Wayne Grady (Calcavecchia won four-hole play-off)	Royal Troon
1990	Nick Faldo	270	5	Mark McNulty, Payne Stewart	St Andrews
1991	Ian Baker-Finch	272	2	Mike Harwood	Royal Birkdale
1992	Nick Faldo	272	1	John Cook	Muirfield
1993	Greg Norman	267	2	Nick Faldo	Sandwich
1994	Nick Price	268	1	Jesper Parnevik	Turnberry
1995	John Daly	282	Play-off	Costantino Rocca (Daly won four-hole play-off)	St Andrews
1996	Tom Lehman	271	2	Mark McCumber, Ernie Els	Royal Lytham
1997	Justin Leonard	272	3	Jesper Parnevik, Darren Clarke	Royal Troon

*Denotes amateurs

Ian Baker-Finch (1991)

Sandy Lyle (1985)

Nick Price (1994)

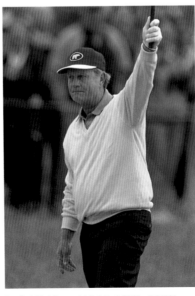

Gary Player (1959, 1968, 1974)   Jack Nicklaus (1966, 1970, 1978)   Greg Norman (1986, 1993)

OPEN CHAMPIONSHIP

MOST VICTORIES
6, Harry Vardon, 1896-98-99-1903-11-14
5, James Braid, 1901-05-06-08-10; J.H. Taylor, 1894-95-1900-09-13; Peter Thomson, 1954-55-56-58-65; Tom Watson, 1975-77-80-82-83

MOST TIMES RUNNER-UP OR JOINT RUNNER-UP
7, Jack Nicklaus, 1964-67-68-72-76-77-79
6, J.H. Taylor, 1896-1904-05-06-07-14

OLDEST WINNER
Old Tom Morris, 46 years 99 days, 1867
Roberto de Vicenzo, 44 years 93 days, 1967

YOUNGEST WINNER
Young Tom Morris, 17 years 5 months 8 days, 1868
Willie Auchterlonie, 21 years 24 days, 1893
Severiano Ballesteros, 22 years 3 months 12 days, 1979

YOUNGEST AND OLDEST COMPETITOR
John Ball, 14 years, 1878
Gene Sarazen, 71 years 4 months 13 days, 1973

BIGGEST MARGIN OF VICTORY
13 strokes, Old Tom Morris, 1862
12 strokes, Young Tom Morris, 1870
8 strokes, J.H. Taylor, 1900 and 1913; James Braid, 1908
6 strokes, Bobby Jones, 1927; Walter Hagen, 1929; Arnold Palmer, 1962; Johnny Miller, 1976

LOWEST WINNING AGGREGATES
267 (66, 68, 69, 64), Greg Norman, Royal St George's, 1993
268 (68, 70, 65, 65), Tom Watson, Turnberry, 1977; (69, 66, 67, 66), Nick Price, Turnberry, 1994
270 (67, 65, 67, 71), Nick Faldo, St Andrews, 1990

LOWEST AGGREGATES BY RUNNER-UP
269 (68, 70, 65, 66), Jack Nicklaus, Turnberry, 1977; (69, 63, 70, 67), Nick Faldo, Royal St George's, 1993; (68, 66, 68, 67), Jesper Parnevik, Turnberry, 1994

LOWEST AGGREGATE BY AN AMATEUR
281 (68, 72, 70, 71), Iain Pyman, Royal St George's, 1993; (75, 66, 70, 70), Tiger Woods, Royal Lytham, 1996

LOWEST INDIVIDUAL ROUND
63, Mark Hayes, second round, Turnberry, 1977; Isao Aoki, third round, Muirfield, 1980; Greg Norman, second round, Turnberry, 1986; Paul Broadhurst, third round, St Andrews, 1990; Jodie Mudd, fourth round, Royal Birkdale, 1991; Nick Faldo, second round, and Payne Stewart, fourth round, Royal St George's, 1993

LOWEST INDIVIDUAL ROUND BY AN AMATEUR
66, Frank Stranahan, fourth round, Troon, 1950; Tiger Woods, second round, Royal Lytham, 1996

LOWEST FIRST ROUND
64, Craig Stadler, Royal Birkdale, 1983; Christy O'Connor Jr., Royal St George's, 1985; Rodger Davis, Muirfield, 1987; Raymond Floyd and Steve Pate, Muirfield, 1992

LOWEST SECOND ROUND
63, Mark Hayes, Turnberry, 1977; Greg Norman, Turnberry, 1986; Nick Faldo, Royal St George's, 1993

LOWEST THIRD ROUND
63, Isao Aoki, Muirfield, 1980; Paul Broadhurst, St Andrews, 1990

LOWEST FOURTH ROUND
63, Jodie Mudd, Royal Birkdale, 1991; Payne Stewart, Royal St George's, 1993

LOWEST FIRST 36 HOLES
130 (66, 64), Nick Faldo, Muirfield, 1992

LOWEST SECOND 36 HOLES
130 (65, 65), Tom Watson, Turnberry, 1977; (64, 66), Ian Baker-Finch, Royal Birkdale, 1991; (66, 64), Anders Forsbrand, Turnberry, 1994

LOWEST FIRST 54 HOLES
198 (67, 67, 64), Tom Lehman, Royal Lytham, 1996

LOWEST FINAL 54 HOLES
199 (66, 67, 66), Nick Price, Turnberry, 1994

LOWEST 9 HOLES
28, Denis Durnian, first 9, Royal Birkdale, 1983
29, Peter Thomson and Tom Haliburton, first 9, Royal

Lytham, 1958; Tony Jacklin, first 9, St Andrews, 1970; Bill Longmuir, first 9, Royal Lytham, 1979; David J. Russell, first 9, Royal Lytham, 1988; Ian Baker-Finch and Paul Broadhurst, first 9, St Andrews, 1990; Ian Baker-Finch, first 9, Royal Birkdale, 1991; Paul McGinley, first 9, Royal Lytham, 1996

CHAMPIONS IN THREE DECADES
Harry Vardon, 1896, 1903, 1911
J.H. Taylor, 1894, 1900, 1913
Gary Player, 1959, 1968, 1974

BIGGEST SPAN BETWEEN FIRST AND LAST VICTORIES
19 years, J.H. Taylor, 1894-1913
18 years, Harry Vardon, 1896-1914
15 years, Gary Player, 1959-74
14 years, Henry Cotton, 1934-48

SUCCESSIVE VICTORIES
4, Young Tom Morris, 1868-72. No championship in 1871
3, Jamie Anderson, 1877-79; Bob Ferguson, 1880-82, Peter Thomson, 1954-56
2, Old Tom Morris, 1861-62; J.H. Taylor, 1894-95; Harry Vardon, 1898-99; James Braid, 1905-06; Bobby Jones, 1926-27; Walter Hagen, 1928-29; Bobby Locke, 1949-50; Arnold Palmer, 1961-62; Lee Trevino, 1971-72; Tom Watson, 1982-83

VICTORIES BY AMATEURS
3, Bobby Jones, 1926-27-30
2, Harold Hilton, 1892-97
1, John Ball, 1890
Roger Wethered lost a play-off in 1921

HIGHEST NUMBER OF TOP FIVE FINISHES
16, J.H. Taylor, Jack Nicklaus
15, Harry Vardon, James Braid

HIGHEST NUMBER OF ROUNDS UNDER 70
33, Jack Nicklaus, Nick Faldo
27, Tom Watson
23, Greg Norman
21, Lee Trevino
20, Severiano Ballesteros

OUTRIGHT LEADER AFTER EVERY ROUND
Willie Auchterlonie, 1893; J.H. Taylor, 1894 and 1900; James Braid, 1908; Ted Ray, 1912; Bobby Jones, 1927; Gene Sarazen, 1932; Henry Cotton, 1934; Tom Weiskopf, 1973

RECORD LEADS (SINCE 1892)
After 18 holes:
4 strokes, James Braid, 1908; Bobby Jones, 1927; Henry Cotton, 1934; Christy O'Connor Jr., 1985
After 36 holes:
9 strokes, Henry Cotton, 1934
After 54 holes:
10 strokes, Henry Cotton, 1934
7 strokes, Tony Lema, 1964
6 strokes, James Braid, 1908; Tom Lehman, 1996

CHAMPIONS WITH EACH ROUND LOWER THAN PREVIOUS ONE
Jack White, 1904, Sandwich, (80, 75, 72, 69)
James Braid, 1906, Muirfield, (77, 76, 74, 73)
Ben Hogan, 1953, Carnoustie, (73, 71, 70, 68)
Gary Player, 1959, Muirfield, (75, 71, 70, 68)

CHAMPION WITH FOUR ROUNDS THE SAME
Densmore Shute, 1933, St Andrews, (73, 73, 73, 73) (excluding the play-off)

BIGGEST VARIATION BETWEEN ROUNDS OF A CHAMPION
14 strokes, Henry Cotton, 1934, second round 65, fourth round 79
11 strokes, Jack White, 1904, first round 80, fourth round 69; Greg Norman, 1986, first round 74, second round 63, third round 74

BIGGEST VARIATION BETWEEN TWO ROUNDS
18 strokes, A. Tingey Jr., 1923, first round 94, second round 76
17 strokes, Jack Nicklaus, 1981, first round 83, second round 66; Ian Baker-Finch, 1986, first round 86, second round 69

BEST COMEBACK BY CHAMPIONS
After 18 holes:
Harry Vardon, 1896, 11 strokes behind the leader
After 36 holes:
George Duncan, 1920, 13 strokes behind the leader
After 54 holes:
Jim Barnes, 1925, 5 strokes behind the leader
Tommy Armour, 1931, 5 strokes behind the leader
Justin Leonard, 1997, 5 strokes behind the leader
Of non-champions, Greg Norman, 1989, 7 strokes behind the leader and lost in a play-off

CHAMPIONS WITH FOUR ROUNDS UNDER 70
Greg Norman, 1993, Royal St George's, (66, 68, 69, 64); Nick Price, 1994, Turnberry, (69, 66, 67, 66)
Of non-champions:
Ernie Els, 1993, Royal St George's, (68, 69, 69, 68); Jesper Parnevik, 1994, Turnberry, (68, 66, 68, 67)

BEST FINISHING ROUND BY A CHAMPION
64, Greg Norman, Royal St George's, 1993
65, Tom Watson, Turnberry, 1977; Severiano Ballesteros, Royal Lytham, 1988; Justin Leonard, Royal Troon, 1997
66, Johnny Miller, Royal Birkdale, 1976; Ian Baker-Finch, Royal Birkdale, 1991; Nick Price, Turnberry, 1994

WORST FINISHING ROUND BY A CHAMPION SINCE 1920
79, Henry Cotton, Sandwich, 1934
78, Reg Whitcombe, Sandwich, 1938
77, Walter Hagen, Hoylake, 1924

WORST OPENING ROUND BY A CHAMPION SINCE 1919
80, George Duncan, Deal, 1920 (he also had a second round of 80)
77, Walter Hagen, Hoylake, 1924

BEST OPENING ROUND BY A CHAMPION
66, Peter Thomson, Royal Lytham, 1958; Nick Faldo, Muirfield, 1992; Greg Norman, Royal St George's, 1993
67, Henry Cotton, Sandwich, 1934; Tom Watson, Royal Birkdale, 1983; Severiano Ballesteros, Royal Lytham, 1988; Nick Faldo, St Andrews, 1990; John Daly, St Andrews, 1995; Tom Lehman, Royal Lytham, 1996

BIGGEST RECOVERY IN 18 HOLES BY A CHAMPION
George Duncan, Deal, 1920, was 13 strokes behind the leader, Abe Mitchell, after 36 holes and level after 54

MOST APPEARANCES ON FINAL DAY (SINCE 1892)
32, Jack Nicklaus
30, J.H. Taylor
27, Harry Vardon, James Braid
26, Peter Thomson, Gary Player
23, Dai Rees
22, Henry Cotton

CHAMPIONSHIP WITH HIGHEST NUMBER OF ROUNDS UNDER 70
148, Turnberry, 1994

CHAMPIONSHIP SINCE 1946 WITH THE FEWEST ROUNDS UNDER 70
St Andrews, 1946; Hoylake, 1947; Portrush, 1951; Hoylake, 1956; Carnoustie, 1968. All had only two rounds under 70

LONGEST COURSE
Carnoustie, 1968, 7252 yd (6631 m)

COURSES MOST OFTEN USED
St Andrews, 25; Prestwick, 24; Muirfield, 14; Sandwich, 12; Hoylake, 10; Royal Lytham, 9; Royal Birkdale and Royal Troon, 7; Musselburgh, 6; Carnoustie, 5; Turnberry, 3; Deal, 2; Royal Portrush and Prince's, 1

PRIZE MONEY

Year	Total	First Prize
1860	nil	nil
1863	10	nil
1864	16	6
1876	27	10
1889	22	8
1891	28.50	10
1892	110	(Amateur winner)
1893	100	30
1910	125	50
1920	225	75
1927	275	100
1930	400	100
1931	500	100
1946	1,000	150
1949	1,700	300
1953	2,450	500
1954	3,500	750
1955	3,750	1,000
1958	4,850	1,000
1959	5,000	1,000
1960	7,000	1,250
1961	8,500	1,400
1963	8,500	1,500
1965	10,000	1,750
1966	15,000	2,100
1968	20,000	3,000
1969	30,000	4,250
1970	40,000	5,250
1971	45,000	5,500
1972	50,000	5,500
1975	75,000	7,500
1977	100,000	10,000
1978	125,000	12,500
1979	155,000	15,500
1980	200,000	25,000
1982	250,000	32,000
1983	300,000	40,000
1984	451,000	55,000
1985	530,000	65,000
1986	600,000	70,000
1987	650,000	75,000
1988	700,000	80,000
1989	750,000	80,000
1990	825,000	85,000
1991	900,000	90,000
1992	950,000	95,000
1993	1,000,000	100,000
1994	1,100,000	110,000
1995	1,250,000	125,000
1996	1,400,000	200,000
1997	1,600,000	250,000

ATTENDANCE

Year	Attendance
1962	37,098
1963	24,585
1964	35,954
1965	32,927
1966	40,182
1967	29,880
1968	51,819
1969	46,001
1970	81,593
1971	70,076
1972	84,746
1973	78,810
1974	92,796
1975	85,258
1976	92,021
1977	87,615
1978	125,271
1979	134,501
1980	131,610
1981	111,987
1982	133,299
1983	142,892
1984	193,126
1985	141,619
1986	134,261
1987	139,189
1988	191,334
1989	160,639
1990	208,680
1991	189,435
1992	146,427
1993	141,000
1994	128,000
1995	180,000
1996	171,000
1997	176,000

COMPLETE SCORES

126TH OPEN CHAMPIONSHIP

*Denotes amateurs

HOLE		1	2	3	4	5	6	7	8	9	10	11	12	13	14	15	16	17	18	TOTAL
PAR		4	4	4	5	3	5	4	3	4	4	4	4	4	3	4	5	3	4	**TOTAL**
Justin Leonard	Round 1	4	3	4	5	3	3	5	3	4	4	4	4	5	3	4	4	3	4	69
USA	Round 2	4	3	4	3	4	3	3	3	4	4	5	4	3	3	4	4	3	5	66
£250,000	Round 3	4	4	4	5	3	5	4	3	4	4	5	5	4	3	4	5	2	4	72
	Round 4	4	3	3	4	4	4	3	3	3	5	4	4	4	3	4	4	2	4	65-272
Darren Clarke	Round 1	4	3	4	4	3	4	3	3	4	5	3	4	4	3	4	4	3	5	67
N. Ireland	Round 2	3	3	4	4	4	4	3	4	3	5	4	4	2	4	4	4	3	4	66
£150,000	Round 3	4	4	3	4	3	4	4	2	4	4	5	4	5	3	5	5	3	5	71
	Round 4	3	6	4	5	3	4	4	3	5	4	4	4	3	5	4	3	3	4	71-275
Jesper Parnevik	Round 1	4	3	4	5	4	4	5	3	4	4	6	4	4	2	5	4	2	3	70
Sweden	Round 2	5	4	4	3	3	5	3	2	4	4	3	4	4	3	4	4	3	4	66
£150,000	Round 3	3	3	4	5	4	4	3	3	4	3	4	5	4	3	4	4	2	4	66
	Round 4	4	4	3	5	3	6	3	3	4	5	3	4	5	3	4	5	4	5	73-275
Jim Furyk	Round 1	3	4	4	4	3	5	3	2	4	4	3	4	5	2	4	5	3	5	67
USA	Round 2	4	4	4	6	3	5	5	2	4	4	4	5	4	3	4	4	3	4	72
£90,000	Round 3	5	4	4	4	4	5	4	4	4	4	3	3	5	3	4	4	2	4	70
	Round 4	4	4	4	5	3	5	4	4	4	4	4	4	3	4	4	3	4	3	70-279
Padraig Harrington	Round 1	4	4	3	4	3	5	4	4	4	4	5	5	5	3	5	5	4	4	75
Ireland	Round 2	4	3	4	5	2	5	4	3	4	4	5	4	3	3	4	5	3	4	69
£62,500	Round 3	4	4	4	4	3	4	4	3	4	4	5	4	3	3	4	5	3	4	69
	Round 4	3	4	3	4	3	4	3	4	4	4	4	3	5	3	5	3	4	4	67-280
Stephen Ames	Round 1	3	4	5	5	3	4	4	5	4	4	4	5	3	5	5	3	4	4	74
Trinidad & Tobago	Round 2	5	3	3	5	4	5	3	3	4	4	3	3	5	3	4	5	3	4	69
£62,500	Round 3	4	3	4	4	3	5	4	3	4	4	4	4	2	3	5	2	4	4	66
	Round 4	5	6	4	5	3	4	4	3	4	3	4	4	3	3	4	5	3	4	71-280
Peter O'Malley	Round 1	3	4	3	4	3	5	4	4	3	4	6	4	4	4	4	5	4	5	73
Australia	Round 2	3	4	3	4	4	5	4	2	4	4	4	5	4	3	4	5	4	4	70
£40,667	Round 3	4	4	4	6	4	5	3	3	4	4	4	4	2	5	5	2	4	3	70
	Round 4	4	4	3	3	3	4	3	4	4	4	4	5	3	4	5	4	4	3	68-281
Eduardo Romero	Round 1	3	4	3	5	3	5	4	2	4	5	4	4	5	4	5	5	4	5	74
Argentina	Round 2	4	3	4	4	2	4	4	3	4	4	5	5	4	3	4	5	2	4	68
£40,667	Round 3	4	4	3	5	2	5	3	3	4	4	5	3	3	3	4	5	2	5	67
	Round 4	4	4	4	5	3	5	3	4	4	4	5	4	3	3	4	5	4	4	72-281

HOLE		1	2	3	4	5	6	7	8	9	10	11	12	13	14	15	16	17	18	
PAR		4	4	4	5	3	5	4	3	4	4	4	4	4	3	4	5	3	4	TOTAL
Fred Couples	Round 1	3	4	4	4	3	4	3	3	3	5	5	4	4	3	4	5	3	5	69
USA	Round 2	3	4	4	4	3	5	4	3	4	4	4	4	4	3	4	5	3	3	68
£40,667	Round 3	4	4	4	5	3	5	4	3	4	4	2	4	4	3	4	5	4	4	70
	Round 4	3	5	4	5	4	4	4	3	4	4	4	5	4	4	5	5	3	4	74-281
Davis Love III	Round 1	3	4	3	4	3	4	4	3	4	4	5	4	4	4	5	5	3	4	70
USA	Round 2	5	4	4	4	3	4	3	4	4	5	4	4	4	3	4	5	3	4	71
£24,300	Round 3	5	4	4	4	4	4	3	7	4	4	5	3	4	3	3	5	4	4	74
	Round 4	4	4	3	4	3	4	4	4	4	4	4	4	4	2	4	5	2	4	67-282
Retief Goosen	Round 1	4	4	4	5	2	4	3	3	5	5	6	4	5	4	5	5	3	4	75
South Africa	Round 2	3	4	4	5	2	5	4	3	4	4	6	4	4	3	4	4	3	3	69
£24,300	Round 3	4	4	4	5	3	5	3	3	5	3	4	4	4	3	4	4	3	5	70
	Round 4	4	3	4	4	3	5	4	3	4	5	5	3	4	2	4	4	3	4	68-282
Frank Nobilo	Round 1	3	4	5	4	3	5	4	3	5	4	4	4	6	3	4	5	4	4	74
New Zealand	Round 2	4	4	4	4	3	5	3	4	4	5	4	4	5	4	4	5	3	3	72
£24,300	Round 3	4	3	4	4	2	5	4	3	4	5	4	3	4	3	4	5	3	4	68
	Round 4	4	3	5	5	3	5	4	2	4	4	3	4	4	2	4	5	3	4	68-282
Tom Kite	Round 1	4	4	3	5	3	5	4	3	4	5	4	4	5	2	5	5	3	4	72
USA	Round 2	3	4	4	4	4	4	4	3	3	5	3	4	3	3	4	5	3	4	67
£24,300	Round 3	4	4	4	6	3	5	4	2	4	4	5	4	5	3	4	5	3	5	74
	Round 4	4	5	3	3	3	4	4	3	3	4	4	5	4	3	5	4	4	4	69-282
Mark Calcavecchia	Round 1	4	4	4	5	2	4	3	5	4	4	4	5	4	4	4	5	3	6	74
USA	Round 2	3	4	3	4	3	5	4	3	4	5	4	5	3	2	4	5	3	3	67
£24,300	Round 3	4	4	4	5	3	5	3	4	4	4	4	4	5	3	4	5	2	5	72
	Round 4	3	4	5	3	3	5	4	4	4	3	4	4	4	3	4	5	3	4	69-282
Shigeki Maruyama	Round 1	4	4	4	4	3	5	4	3	4	4	6	5	5	3	4	5	3	4	74
Japan	Round 2	4	4	4	4	3	5	4	3	4	5	3	4	4	5	4	2	3	69
£24,300	Round 3	4	4	3	4	3	6	4	3	4	4	4	4	5	3	4	4	3	4	70
	Round 4	4	4	4	4	3	5	3	3	4	4	4	4	4	3	4	5	3	4	69-282
Ernie Els	Round 1	4	4	4	4	3	5	4	3	4	6	4	4	4	3	5	5	4	5	75
South Africa	Round 2	4	4	5	4	3	5	5	2	3	4	4	4	4	3	4	5	2	4	69
£24,300	Round 3	3	4	4	4	4	4	3	2	5	4	4	5	4	3	4	5	3	4	69
	Round 4	3	5	4	4	3	4	3	3	3	3	5	6	4	3	4	5	3	4	69-282
Tom Watson	Round 1	3	4	4	4	3	4	4	3	4	5	4	4	5	3	4	5	4	4	71
USA	Round 2	3	3	4	5	3	4	3	4	4	5	4	5	3	3	5	4	3	5	70
£24,300	Round 3	5	4	4	5	3	5	3	4	4	4	4	4	4	3	4	4	2	4	70
	Round 4	4	4	4	4	3	4	3	5	5	4	5	4	4	3	4	4	4	3	71-282
Lee Westwood	Round 1	3	4	4	4	3	5	4	4	5	4	5	4	5	3	4	5	3	4	73
England	Round 2	4	4	3	3	3	5	4	2	4	5	4	5	4	4	4	5	3	4	70
£24,300	Round 3	5	3	4	4	3	4	3	2	4	5	4	5	4	2	4	5	2	4	67
	Round 4	3	4	4	6	2	6	4	4	4	3	4	4	4	3	4	6	2	5	72-282
Robert Allenby	Round 1	4	4	4	5	3	5	4	4	5	4	5	4	5	3	5	5	3	4	76
Australia	Round 2	4	4	4	3	3	4	4	2	3	4	5	4	4	3	5	5	3	4	68
£24,300	Round 3	3	4	4	4	3	5	3	4	4	4	3	4	5	2	4	4	3	3	66
	Round 4	3	4	4	4	4	5	4	3	3	4	7	4	4	3	4	5	3	4	72-282
Jose Maria Olazabal	Round 1	4	4	3	5	3	6	3	3	4	6	5	4	5	3	5	5	3	4	75
Spain	Round 2	4	4	3	4	3	4	3	4	3	4	4	5	4	3	3	5	3	5	68
£14,500	Round 3	4	4	4	4	3	4	4	3	4	5	5	5	5	3	4	5	3	4	73
	Round 4	4	3	4	5	3	5	3	2	4	4	4	4	4	3	4	4	3	4	67-283

HOLE		1	2	3	4	5	6	7	8	9	10	11	12	13	14	15	16	17	18	
PAR		4	4	4	5	3	5	4	3	4	4	4	4	4	3	4	5	3	4	TOTAL
Brad Faxon	Round 1	3	4	5	6	3	5	5	2	5	6	4	4	5	3	5	4	3	5	77
USA	Round 2	3	4	3	4	3	5	4	2	4	4	4	3	4	3	5	5	3	4	67
£14,500	Round 3	3	4	4	4	3	5	4	3	4	6	4	5	4	3	5	4	3	4	72
	Round 4	4	5	4	4	3	4	4	2	4	4	4	3	4	2	4	4	3	5	67-283
Mark James	Round 1	4	4	5	4	3	5	4	3	4	5	5	4	5	4	5	4	4	4	76
England	Round 2	4	4	3	4	4	5	4	3	3	5	3	3	4	2	5	4	3	4	67
£14,500	Round 3	3	4	4	4	3	6	4	3	4	5	4	4	3	4	5	3	3	70
	Round 4	4	4	4	3	3	4	4	3	4	5	5	4	4	3	4	5	3	4	70-283
Stuart Appleby	Round 1	4	3	4	4	3	4	4	4	4	5	4	5	5	2	5	4	3	5	72
Australia	Round 2	4	4	4	5	3	4	3	3	5	4	5	4	4	3	5	5	3	4	72
£14,500	Round 3	4	4	4	3	2	4	4	3	4	4	5	4	4	4	5	4	2	4	68
	Round 4	4	4	4	5	4	4	4	3	4	5	4	4	3	3	3	5	4	4	71-283
Tom Lehman	Round 1	4	4	4	4	2	5	4	3	4	5	4	5	4	3	5	5	4	5	74
USA	Round 2	4	7	4	4	2	5	4	2	4	4	4	4	4	3	4	5	4	4	72
£10,363	Round 3	4	4	4	4	3	4	4	2	4	4	5	4	5	3	5	6	3	4	72
	Round 4	3	4	4	4	3	5	3	3	4	4	4	4	3	3	4	3	4	66-284
David A. Russell	Round 1	4	4	4	4	3	4	4	3	5	5	5	4	2	5	6	4	5	75
England	Round 2	3	4	5	5	3	5	3	3	4	4	4	5	5	2	4	5	4	4	72
£10,363	Round 3	4	4	4	4	3	5	3	3	3	4	4	5	4	3	4	4	2	5	68
	Round 4	4	5	3	4	3	4	5	3	5	4	4	4	5	2	4	4	2	4	69-284
Jay Haas	Round 1	4	3	4	5	3	5	4	2	4	5	3	4	4	4	4	5	3	5	71
USA	Round 2	4	4	4	4	3	4	4	2	3	5	4	4	5	3	5	5	3	4	70
£10,363	Round 3	4	4	4	4	3	5	4	3	4	4	5	5	4	3	4	4	4	5	73
	Round 4	4	3	4	5	2	4	4	3	4	4	4	5	4	4	4	5	3	4	70-284
Colin Montgomerie	Round 1	4	4	4	4	3	4	5	4	5	5	4	5	5	3	5	5	3	4	76
Scotland	Round 2	4	3	5	4	2	3	4	3	3	4	4	4	5	3	4	5	5	4	69
£10,363	Round 3	3	4	4	5	3	5	4	2	4	4	4	4	4	3	4	5	3	4	69
	Round 4	4	4	3	4	3	5	4	5	5	4	4	3	3	3	4	5	3	4	70-284
Phil Mickelson	Round 1	4	5	4	4	3	4	4	3	4	4	5	5	5	3	5	5	4	5	76
USA	Round 2	3	4	4	4	3	5	4	2	3	5	4	4	5	3	4	5	3	3	68
£10,363	Round 3	3	4	4	4	3	4	5	3	4	5	5	4	2	4	5	3	3	69
	Round 4	4	3	3	4	4	6	4	3	4	5	4	4	4	4	4	5	3	3	71-284
Ian Woosnam	Round 1	5	4	5	4	4	4	4	2	3	4	5	4	5	3	4	4	3	4	71
Wales	Round 2	3	4	4	5	3	4	4	3	4	5	4	4	4	4	4	5	4	5	73
£10,363	Round 3	4	4	4	4	3	5	3	3	4	4	4	4	3	4	5	3	4	69
	Round 4	4	4	4	4	2	5	4	2	4	4	7	6	3	3	4	4	3	4	71-284
Peter Lonard	Round 1	3	4	4	4	3	4	4	2	4	5	5	4	5	3	5	5	4	4	72
Australia	Round 2	4	4	4	5	2	5	4	3	4	4	4	4	4	3	4	5	3	4	70
£10,363	Round 3	4	4	4	4	2	5	4	3	4	4	5	4	4	2	4	5	3	4	69
	Round 4	5	4	4	4	4	5	4	3	4	4	4	4	4	3	4	5	4	4	73-284
Tiger Woods	Round 1	4	4	4	4	3	4	4	4	4	4	7	4	5	3	4	4	3	3	72
USA	Round 2	4	4	5	4	4	4	4	3	4	8	4	4	4	3	4	5	3	3	74
£10,363	Round 3	3	3	4	4	4	4	3	3	4	4	5	3	4	3	4	3	2	4	64
	Round 4	4	4	4	4	2	5	4	6	4	4	4	5	4	3	4	5	3	5	74-284
Mark McNulty	Round 1	4	4	4	4	4	5	4	5	3	6	7	4	4	3	4	5	3	5	78
Zimbabwe	Round 2	3	4	4	4	3	5	3	2	4	5	3	4	4	4	4	4	3	4	67
£8,320	Round 3	4	4	4	5	3	3	4	3	4	5	5	4	5	2	5	5	3	4	72
	Round 4	4	4	4	3	4	4	3	3	4	4	5	4	4	3	4	4	4	4	69-286

HOLE		1	2	3	4	5	6	7	8	9	10	11	12	13	14	15	16	17	18	
PAR		4	4	4	5	3	5	4	3	4	4	4	4	4	3	4	5	3	4	TOTAL
Andrew Magee	Round 1	4	4	4	4	3	4	4	3	4	5	4	4	4	4	4	5	2	4	70
USA	Round 2	4	5	4	5	6	5	5	2	4	3	4	4	4	3	4	6	3	4	75
£8,320	Round 3	6	4	5	4	3	5	4	3	4	5	4	3	4	3	5	5	2	3	72
	Round 4	4	4	4	4	4	4	4	2	3	4	5	4	4	3	5	4	3	4	69-286
Rodger Davis	Round 1	4	4	3	4	4	4	4	3	4	4	4	4	5	3	4	5	6	4	73
Australia	Round 2	4	3	4	4	4	5	5	3	3	5	5	4	5	3	4	5	3	4	73
£8,320	Round 3	4	4	4	5	2	5	3	4	3	4	4	4	4	3	5	5	3	4	70
	Round 4	3	4	4	5	3	4	3	3	4	4	5	5	5	3	4	5	3	3	70-286
David Duval	Round 1	4	4	4	4	3	5	3	3	4	5	6	4	5	3	4	4	4	4	73
USA	Round 2	5	4	3	3	3	4	4	3	3	5	4	5	4	3	4	4	3	5	69
£8,320	Round 3	3	4	4	5	4	5	3	3	5	5	4	5	4	2	4	5	5	3	73
	Round 4	3	5	4	5	3	4	4	2	4	4	6	5	5	3	4	4	3	3	71-286
Jonathan Lomas	Round 1	4	4	4	5	3	4	4	2	4	6	5	5	4	3	5	4	2	4	72
England	Round 2	3	4	4	4	4	4	3	3	5	5	4	4	4	3	4	5	3	5	71
£8,320	Round 3	3	4	4	3	3	5	4	2	5	4	5	4	4	3	4	5	4	3	69
	Round 4	4	4	4	4	3	5	3	5	4	4	5	4	5	3	4	4	4	5	74-286
Greg Norman	Round 1	4	4	3	4	4	4	3	3	3	4	4	4	5	3	4	5	3	5	69
Australia	Round 2	4	4	4	5	3	4	4	3	4	5	5	4	4	3	4	5	3	5	73
£7,900	Round 3	4	4	4	4	3	5	3	2	4	5	4	4	4	3	5	5	3	4	70
	Round 4	4	4	4	4	3	5	5	3	4	4	4	5	5	4	6	4	3	4	75-287
Mark O'Meara	Round 1	4	4	4	5	3	4	4	3	4	4	4	4	5	5	3	4	5	3	73
USA	Round 2	4	4	5	5	3	4	4	4	4	4	4	4	5	4	3	4	5	3	73
£7,550	Round 3	4	3	5	5	3	4	4	3	4	5	4	5	5	3	4	5	4	4	74
	Round 4	3	3	4	4	3	5	5	2	4	4	4	3	4	3	5	4	4	4	68-288
John Kernohan	Round 1	5	4	4	5	3	4	4	2	4	5	4	5	6	4	5	5	4	3	76
USA	Round 2	3	4	4	5	3	5	4	3	3	4	5	4	4	3	5	4	3	4	70
£7,550	Round 3	3	6	4	4	3	5	4	3	4	5	4	4	5	2	5	5	3	5	74
	Round 4	4	4	3	5	3	4	4	2	4	3	5	4	4	3	4	5	2	5	68-288
Raymond Russell	Round 1	4	4	4	4	3	5	3	2	4	5	5	3	5	3	5	5	3	6	72
Scotland	Round 2	4	4	3	4	3	6	4	4	4	4	4	4	4	3	4	4	5	4	72
£7,550	Round 3	5	4	4	4	3	5	4	2	4	4	5	6	4	3	5	5	3	4	74
	Round 4	5	4	4	5	3	4	5	2	4	3	5	4	4	2	4	5	3	4	70-288
Michael Bradley	Round 1	4	4	3	5	4	4	4	3	4	4	5	4	4	3	5	5	3	4	72
USA	Round 2	4	4	4	4	3	6	4	2	4	5	5	3	5	3	5	5	4	3	73
£7,550	Round 3	4	4	4	4	3	6	4	3	4	5	4	5	4	3	4	4	4	4	73
	Round 4	4	4	4	4	3	6	3	3	3	4	4	4	4	4	4	5	3	4	70-288
Vijay Singh	Round 1	5	4	5	4	3	4	4	3	4	5	5	5	5	5	3	5	4	4	77
Fiji	Round 2	4	4	4	5	3	4	4	3	4	5	4	4	3	3	4	5	2	4	69
£7,550	Round 3	3	3	4	4	3	5	4	3	4	4	4	6	4	3	5	4	3	4	70
	Round 4	4	4	4	4	3	4	4	4	4	4	6	3	4	3	5	5	3	4	72-288
Bernhard Langer	Round 1	4	4	4	4	3	4	4	2	4	4	4	4	5	3	5	5	3	6	72
Germany	Round 2	4	4	4	5	3	5	4	3	4	4	5	4	4	3	6	5	2	5	74
£7,550	Round 3	3	4	4	5	3	5	4	3	4	4	5	3	4	2	4	5	3	4	69
	Round 4	4	4	4	5	3	5	5	3	5	5	4	4	5	2	4	5	2	4	73-288
Jose Coceres	Round 1	3	4	4	4	4	5	4	3	5	5	5	4	5	4	5	5	3	4	76
Argentina	Round 2	4	4	3	5	3	5	4	3	4	4	4	3	4	3	4	6	3	4	70
£7,050	Round 3	4	4	4	5	3	4	4	2	4	4	4	4	5	2	5	5	4	4	71
	Round 4	4	5	4	5	4	4	3	4	4	5	4	4	4	3	4	4	4	3	72-289

HOLE		1	2	3	4	5	6	7	8	9	10	11	12	13	14	15	16	17	18	
PAR		4	4	4	5	3	5	4	3	4	4	4	4	4	3	4	5	3	4	TOTAL
Jerry Kelly	Round 1	4	4	5	5	3	4	4	3	4	5	4	5	4	4	5	5	3	5	76
USA	Round 2	4	5	3	4	3	4	4	3	4	4	4	4	4	2	4	5	3	4	68
£7,050	Round 3	4	4	4	4	3	5	3	3	4	4	4	4	4	4	4	5	4	5	72
	Round 4	5	4	3	5	3	5	4	3	3	5	4	5	4	3	4	5	4	4	73-289
David Tapping	Round 1	3	4	4	4	3	5	4	3	4	4	4	5	5	3	3	5	3	5	71
England	Round 2	4	3	4	5	3	4	4	2	4	3	3	5	4	3	3	5	3	4	66
£7,050	Round 3	4	5	5	5	4	5	3	3	4	5	5	4	4	5	5	5	3	4	78
	Round 4	3	4	5	5	3	5	4	3	3	4	6	4	6	3	4	4	4	4	74-289
Curtis Strange	Round 1	3	4	4	5	3	5	4	3	4	4	4	4	4	2	5	5	3	5	71
USA	Round 2	5	4	4	5	3	4	4	4	4	4	4	4	3	3	3	6	3	4	71
£7,050	Round 3	4	4	4	4	2	4	4	3	4	4	5	4	5	2	4	5	4	4	70
	Round 4	4	5	4	5	3	4	4	3	4	5	4	4	4	4	5	6	4	5	77-289
Jim Payne	Round 1	4	4	3	4	4	4	4	4	4	5	4	5	4	3	4	5	4	5	74
England	Round 2	5	3	4	4	3	4	3	3	4	5	4	4	4	3	5	5	3	5	71
£6,750	Round 3	5	4	3	4	3	5	3	4	5	4	4	5	4	4	5	5	3	4	74
	Round 4	5	3	4	4	3	6	3	2	4	4	4	4	5	3	3	5	4	5	71-290
Steve Jones	Round 1	4	4	4	5	2	4	4	3	7	5	4	5	5	3	4	5	3	5	76
USA	Round 2	3	4	4	5	3	4	4	3	4	5	4	5	4	4	4	5	3	3	71
£6,750	Round 3	4	3	4	5	3	4	3	2	4	5	4	5	4	3	4	4	3	4	68
	Round 4	3	4	4	4	3	4	6	4	5	4	4	4	5	2	4	5	3	7	75-290
Corey Pavin	Round 1	4	5	4	4	3	7	3	3	3	5	5	6	5	3	5	5	3	5	78
USA	Round 2	4	4	3	4	3	4	4	3	4	5	4	4	4	3	4	5	3	4	69
£6,206	Round 3	4	4	5	5	2	4	4	2	4	6	6	4	5	3	5	5	3	5	76
	Round 4	5	4	3	4	3	4	3	3	4	4	4	4	5	2	4	5	3	4	68-291
Peter Mitchell	Round 1	4	4	4	5	4	5	4	3	3	5	4	4	5	3	5	5	3	5	75
England	Round 2	4	4	4	4	3	4	4	2	4	4	5	3	4	3	4	5	3	5	69
£6,206	Round 3	4	4	4	5	3	5	4	3	4	4	5	4	5	4	5	5	4	4	76
	Round 4	3	4	4	4	3	6	4	4	4	4	4	4	4	3	5	5	3	3	71-291
Wayne Riley	Round 1	4	4	4	5	3	4	4	2	4	6	4	4	6	3	5	5	3	4	74
Australia	Round 2	4	4	4	6	3	4	4	2	3	4	4	5	3	4	5	3	4	71
£6,206	Round 3	4	4	4	5	3	5	6	3	4	5	5	5	4	3	4	5	3	3	75
	Round 4	4	5	4	5	2	4	4	2	4	4	4	4	4	4	5	5	3	4	71-291
Nick Faldo	Round 1	4	5	4	4	3	4	4	3	5	5	4	4	4	3	4	5	3	3	71
England	Round 2	4	4	4	7	3	4	4	3	4	4	4	4	4	3	4	5	3	5	73
£6,206	Round 3	5	4	4	4	4	3	5	3	4	5	6	4	6	3	4	4	3	4	75
	Round 4	4	4	4	4	3	5	5	4	5	4	5	4	4	3	4	5	2	3	72-291
Peter Senior	Round 1	3	4	5	4	3	5	4	3	4	6	6	4	4	3	5	6	3	4	76
Australia	Round 2	4	5	4	5	3	4	3	4	3	4	4	4	5	2	4	5	3	4	70
£6,206	Round 3	4	5	4	4	3	4	4	4	4	4	4	4	5	4	4	5	2	5	73
	Round 4	5	4	4	4	3	6	4	3	3	4	4	4	4	3	5	5	3	4	72-291
Greg Turner	Round 1	4	4	4	5	2	5	4	3	4	5	5	5	4	4	5	4	4	5	76
New Zealand	Round 2	4	4	3	5	3	5	3	4	4	5	4	4	4	3	4	5	3	4	71
£6,206	Round 3	4	5	3	4	3	5	4	3	4	4	4	4	5	3	4	5	4	4	72
	Round 4	4	4	4	3	3	6	5	3	4	4	4	4	4	3	5	5	3	4	72-291
Richard Boxall	Round 1	4	4	4	4	3	5	4	3	3	4	5	4	5	4	5	6	4	4	75
England	Round 2	4	5	3	3	4	5	4	3	4	5	4	4	5	2	4	5	3	4	71
£6,206	Round 3	4	4	4	5	3	4	3	3	3	5	5	4	4	3	6	4	4	4	72
	Round 4	4	4	4	4	4	5	4	3	3	5	4	4	5	4	4	6	3	3	73-291

HOLE		1	2	3	4	5	6	7	8	9	10	11	12	13	14	15	16	17	18	
PAR		4	4	4	5	3	5	4	3	4	4	4	4	4	3	4	5	3	4	TOTAL
Angel Cabrera	Round 1	3	5	4	4	3	4	4	4	4	3	4	3	6	3	4	5	3	4	70
Argentina	Round 2	5	4	4	5	4	5	3	2	3	4	5	3	5	3	4	4	3	4	70
£6,206	Round 3	3	3	4	4	4	6	3	4	4	4	8	4	5	3	4	5	3	5	76
	Round 4	4	4	4	4	4	5	4	6	4	5	4	4	5	3	4	5	2	4	75-291
Jeff Maggert	Round 1	5	4	5	5	3	4	4	3	4	4	4	4	4	4	4	5	4	6	76
USA	Round 2	4	3	3	4	3	4	4	3	5	5	5	3	5	4	3	5	3	3	69
£6,206	Round 3	3	4	3	6	3	6	3	3	4	5	4	4	2	4	5	4	4	4	71
	Round 4	4	4	4	4	3	5	4	4	5	5	4	4	3	4	5	5	4	4	75-291
Payne Stewart	Round 1	3	4	4	4	2	4	4	3	5	5	5	4	5	4	5	5	3	4	73
USA	Round 2	4	3	5	3	3	5	4	3	4	4	4	4	5	4	4	5	6	4	74
£5,800	Round 3	4	4	4	5	3	5	4	2	4	4	4	4	4	4	4	5	3	4	71
	Round 4	6	4	4	5	3	5	4	3	3	4	4	4	4	3	4	6	4	4	74-292
***Barclay Howard**	Round 1	3	3	4	4	3	4	4	3	4	5	5	3	5	3	4	5	3	5	70
Scotland	Round 2	4	4	4	4	2	5	5	3	4	5	5	4	4	4	5	5	4	4	74
Silver Medal	Round 3	4	4	4	4	4	4	4	3	4	4	4	4	3	7	5	5	5	5	76
	Round 4	5	5	4	4	4	5	4	2	4	4	4	4	4	4	5	4	3	4	73-293
Jack Nicklaus	Round 1	5	4	5	4	3	5	4	3	5	4	5	4	5	2	4	4	3	4	73
USA	Round 2	4	4	4	5	3	5	4	4	5	4	4	4	3	4	5	4	3	5	74
£5,750	Round 3	4	4	4	4	2	3	4	3	4	4	5	4	5	4	5	5	4	3	71
	Round 4	4	4	4	4	3	4	4	4	5	5	5	5	4	3	5	5	3	5	75-293
Steve Stricker	Round 1	3	5	4	4	3	4	4	3	4	4	5	3	5	3	4	4	5	5	72
USA	Round 2	3	4	4	4	3	5	4	4	5	6	5	3	5	2	4	5	3	4	73
£5,625	Round 3	4	4	4	4	4	5	4	2	4	5	7	4	4	2	4	4	5	4	74
	Round 4	4	4	5	5	4	5	4	3	4	4	4	4	5	4	5	4	3	4	75-294
Peter Teravainen	Round 1	4	4	4	5	3	5	4	3	3	4	5	4	5	3	5	4	3	6	74
USA	Round 2	4	5	3	5	4	4	4	2	4	5	5	3	4	3	5	5	3	4	72
£5,625	Round 3	4	3	4	4	3	4	4	4	4	5	4	4	3	4	6	4	4	5	73
	Round 4	4	4	4	3	3	5	3	2	4	4	8	4	4	3	6	5	4	5	75-294
Jamie Spence	Round 1	5	5	4	5	3	5	5	3	4	5	4	4	5	3	5	5	4	4	78
England	Round 2	4	3	4	4	4	5	4	2	4	4	4	4	4	3	4	5	3	4	69
£5,625	Round 3	4	3	4	5	3	4	4	4	4	4	5	5	5	2	4	4	3	5	72
	Round 4	6	4	4	4	3	4	4	4	4	4	4	5	4	3	5	4	5	4	75-294
Tom Purtzer	Round 1	4	4	4	4	3	5	3	4	4	4	4	4	5	3	5	5	3	4	72
USA	Round 2	4	3	4	5	3	4	4	2	4	4	5	4	4	4	5	5	3	4	71
£5,625	Round 3	4	5	4	6	3	5	4	3	4	4	4	4	5	2	4	5	3	4	73
	Round 4	4	5	4	4	3	7	5	3	4	3	6	5	5	4	5	4	3	4	78-294
Paul McGinley	Round 1	4	4	5	5	3	5	3	3	4	5	5	4	4	3	5	6	3	5	76
Ireland	Round 2	3	4	5	5	4	5	3	2	4	4	5	4	4	3	5	4	3	4	71
£5,450	Round 3	4	4	4	5	4	6	4	3	4	5	4	4	5	4	5	5	3	4	77
	Round 4	4	4	4	4	3	5	4	2	5	4	5	4	4	3	4	5	3	4	71-295
Per-Ulrik Johansson	Round 1	4	5	4	3	3	4	4	3	4	7	4	5	4	2	4	5	3	4	72
Sweden	Round 2	4	3	3	5	3	4	5	5	4	4	4	4	4	5	5	4	3	6	75
£5,450	Round 3	4	4	4	4	4	4	4	6	5	3	3	4	4	3	4	5	4	4	73
	Round 4	4	4	4	4	4	5	4	5	4	3	6	4	5	3	5	5	2	4	75-295
Gary Clark	Round 1	4	4	4	4	2	4	4	4	4	5	5	4	5	3	5	6	3	4	74
England	Round 2	4	4	4	4	2	4	6	3	4	5	5	4	4	3	5	4	3	4	72
£5,450	Round 3	4	3	4	4	3	5	4	4	4	4	4	4	4	3	3	5	4	6	72
	Round 4	4	6	4	4	3	5	4	4	5	4	3	4	5	3	5	5	4	5	77-295

HOLE		1	2	3	4	5	6	7	8	9	10	11	12	13	14	15	16	17	18	
PAR		4	4	4	5	3	5	4	3	4	4	4	4	4	3	4	5	3	4	TOTAL
Tommy Tolles	Round 1	2	5	4	4	4	6	4	4	3	4	5	5	4	4	4	6	4	5	77
USA	Round 2	3	4	4	4	3	5	4	2	4	4	4	4	3	4	5	3	4		68
£5,350	Round 3	6	3	5	4	3	4	4	5	4	5	5	4	3	4	4	5	3	4	75
	Round 4	3	4	4	6	4	5	4	4	4	4	4	4	5	3	5	4	4	5	76-296
Billy Andrade	Round 1	4	4	4	5	3	4	4	4	3	5	4	4	4	3	4	5	4	4	72
USA	Round 2	3	4	5	5	4	5	3	3	4	4	5	4	4	2	5	4	4	4	72
£5,300	Round 3	4	4	6	5	3	5	4	3	4	6	4	5	4	3	6	4	4	4	78
	Round 4	4	4	4	5	4	6	5	3	4	4	6	3	4	4	4	5	3	4	76-298

NON QUALIFIERS AFTER 36 HOLES

(Leading 10 professionals and ties receive £1,000 each, next 20 professionals and ties receive £800 each, next 20 professionals and ties receive £700 each, remainder of professionals receive £650 each.)

Player	Round	1	2	3	4	5	6	7	8	9	10	11	12	13	14	15	16	17	18	TOTAL
Gary Orr	Round 1	3	4	3	4	4	4	6	4	4	4	6	4	4	3	6	5	4	4	76
Scotland	Round 2	4	4	4	5	2	5	3	3	4	4	5	4	4	2	4	5	4	6	72-148
Mark Wiebe	Round 1	4	4	4	4	3	4	4	3	6	5	4	4	4	2	5	5	4	4	73
USA	Round 2	4	5	3	4	2	7	4	3	4	4	5	5	5	3	4	5	4	4	75-148
Michael Long	Round 1	4	4	4	5	3	5	4	3	4	5	6	5	6	4	5	4	3	4	78
New Zealand	Round 2	4	6	4	4	3	5	4	3	3	3	4	4	4	3	4	5	3	4	70-148
Steve Elkington	Round 1	4	3	4	6	3	5	5	5	4	3	4	5	5	2	5	5	4	4	76
Australia	Round 2	4	4	4	4	3	5	4	3	5	5	5	4	4	3	4	4	3	4	72-148
Peter Hedblom	Round 1	3	4	4	6	3	4	3	2	4	5	4	8	5	3	4	6	4	4	76
Sweden	Round 2	4	4	5	5	3	5	3	3	3	5	4	4	4	4	5	4	3	4	72-148
Gordon Brand Jnr	Round 1	4	5	4	4	3	5	5	3	4	6	5	4	5	3	4	5	3	4	76
Scotland	Round 2	4	3	4	4	3	3	5	4	5	4	4	4	4	4	5	5	3	4	72-148
Carl Mason	Round 1	4	4	3	6	4	5	4	3	5	4	5	4	5	4	5	4	3	6	78
England	Round 2	3	4	5	5	3	4	4	3	4	4	4	4	4	3	4	5	3	4	70-148
Pierre Fulke	Round 1	4	3	4	4	3	4	4	3	5	5	4	5	5	1	4	6	5	4	73
Sweden	Round 2	4	4	3	4	3	6	4	3	4	4	5	4	5	4	5	5	3	5	75-148
David Howell	Round 1	3	3	6	5	3	6	4	3	4	5	4	4	5	5	3	5	3	4	75
England	Round 2	3	3	3	4	3	4	4	3	4	5	6	4	5	4	4	5	3	6	73-148
Wayne Westner	Round 1	3	4	5	5	3	5	4	3	4	4	5	5	5	3	4	5	4	4	75
South Africa	Round 2	4	5	4	5	3	5	4	3	4	5	4	4	3	2	5	5	3	5	73-148
Andrew Coltart	Round 1	4	4	4	5	4	5	5	3	4	4	5	4	4	4	5	5	3	5	76
Scotland	Round 2	4	3	4	4	3	5	4	3	5	4	4	4	4	3	6	5	3	4	72-148
Dean Robertson	Round 1	4	4	4	4	3	4	4	5	5	5	5	4	4	3	4	5	3	5	76
Scotland	Round 2	3	3	3	5	2	4	4	4	4	4	5	5	4	4	4	7	3	4	72-148
Severiano Ballesteros	Round 1	3	5	5	4	3	4	4	3	5	4	6	4	5	3	4	6	4	5	77
Spain	Round 2	4	3	4	6	3	4	4	3	4	5	4	3	5	3	4	5	3	4	71-148
Paul Curry	Round 1	4	4	5	4	3	5	4	3	5	5	5	4	5	4	4	5	4	6	79
England	Round 2	4	3	4	3	2	5	3	5	4	5	5	3	4	2	4	6	3	4	69-148
Robert Karlsson	Round 1	4	3	4	4	4	5	3	4	4	5	6	4	5	3	4	5	4	5	76
Sweden	Round 2	4	3	4	5	3	5	4	2	4	4	5	4	4	3	5	5	3	5	72-148
Lee Janzen	Round 1	4	3	4	4	4	4	4	3	5	5	5	5	6	3	5	7	3	4	78
USA	Round 2	3	4	4	4	3	6	3	3	5	4	4	4	4	3	4	5	3	5	71-149
Craig Parry	Round 1	4	4	5	5	4	4	4	6	3	5	5	5	6	3	4	5	3	4	79
Australia	Round 2	4	4	4	4	3	4	3	4	5	4	4	4	5	3	4	4	3	4	70-149
Craig Stadler	Round 1	4	4	5	4	4	4	6	3	5	5	4	5	5	3	5	4	4	4	78
USA	Round 2	3	4	4	4	4	4	6	3	4	3	5	4	5	3	4	4	3	4	71-149

HOLE		1	2	3	4	5	6	7	8	9	10	11	12	13	14	15	16	17	18	
PAR		4	4	4	5	3	5	4	3	4	4	4	4	4	3	4	5	3	4	TOTAL
Gary Player	Round 1	4	4	5	5	2	5	5	4	5	4	5	4	4	3	5	6	4	4	78
South Africa	Round 2	3	4	4	5	3	4	3	3	3	5	5	4	5	3	4	5	3	5	71-149
Robert Damron	Round 1	5	4	4	4	3	5	4	4	3	4	6	4	4	4	4	5	4	5	76
USA	Round 2	4	5	4	3	3	5	4	4	3	5	5	4	5	3	3	5	3	5	73-149
Peter Baker	Round 1	4	4	6	6	2	4	4	4	4	5	6	4	4	4	5	5	4	4	79
England	Round 2	4	4	5	5	3	4	4	2	4	4	4	4	4	3	4	4	3	5	70-149
Brian Watts	Round 1	4	4	3	5	3	5	4	3	5	4	5	4	5	3	5	5	4	4	75
USA	Round 2	3	4	4	6	3	5	5	3	3	5	5	4	3	4	4	6	3	4	74-149
*Craig Watson	Round 1	3	3	4	6	4	4	4	2	4	4	5	4	5	4	4	5	4	4	73
Scotland	Round 2	4	5	4	4	2	4	4	3	4	4	5	4	5	4	4	6	5	5	76-149
Thomas Bjorn	Round 1	3	5	4	4	3	5	5	3	4	5	4	5	3	5	5	5	3	5	76
Denmark	Round 2	4	4	4	5	3	5	4	3	4	5	4	4	3	4	4	5	4	4	73-149
Paul Broadhurst	Round 1	4	4	4	4	3	5	4	3	4	5	4	5	4	3	4	6	3	5	75
England	Round 2	4	4	4	4	3	5	4	3	4	4	5	4	4	3	5	6	3	5	74-149
Loren Roberts	Round 1	4	4	4	5	2	6	5	2	4	5	5	4	5	4	4	4	4	5	76
USA	Round 2	4	4	5	5	3	5	4	2	4	5	4	4	2	4	5	4	5	5	73-149
Costantino Rocca	Round 1	4	4	4	4	3	4	3	4	5	5	4	5	4	3	5	5	4	5	75
Italy	Round 2	4	4	4	5	3	5	4	3	4	5	5	4	4	3	4	5	3	6	75-150
Mark Brooks	Round 1	6	4	4	5	3	4	5	3	4	5	4	5	4	3	5	4	6	6	80
USA	Round 2	4	3	4	4	3	5	4	3	4	5	4	4	4	3	4	5	3	4	70-150
Nick Price	Round 1	4	4	4	5	3	6	5	2	5	6	4	4	6	3	5	4	4	4	78
Zimbabwe	Round 2	4	3	4	6	4	5	4	3	4	4	4	4	5	3	4	5	2	4	72-150
Glen Day	Round 1	4	5	4	5	3	4	7	2	4	4	5	4	3	4	4	6	4	6	78
USA	Round 2	4	4	4	5	2	5	5	3	5	4	4	4	3	3	5	4	4	4	72-150
Scott Dunlap	Round 1	4	4	5	4	3	5	4	2	4	5	7	4	4	3	5	5	4	5	77
USA	Round 2	4	4	4	4	3	5	4	3	5	5	4	4	5	3	4	6	3	3	73-150
Scott McCarron	Round 1	4	4	4	5	4	3	4	2	4	4	6	4	4	4	4	5	3	5	73
USA	Round 2	4	4	5	5	3	5	5	3	4	5	5	5	4	3	5	5	4	4	77-150
Ignacio Garrido	Round 1	4	4	4	5	4	4	4	3	6	7	4	4	6	4	5	4	3	4	79
Spain	Round 2	4	4	4	5	4	4	4	2	5	5	4	4	3	3	4	5	4	4	72-151
Miguel Angel Martin	Round 1	6	4	5	5	4	5	4	5	4	4	4	4	4	4	4	5	3	5	79
Spain	Round 2	4	4	4	4	3	5	3	3	3	4	5	4	4	3	6	4	4	5	72-151
Joost Steenkamer	Round 1	3	4	5	5	3	5	4	4	3	5	5	4	7	3	4	5	4	5	78
The Netherlands	Round 2	4	4	4	4	2	5	4	2	4	5	4	5	5	3	4	7	3	4	73-151
Philip Blackmar	Round 1	4	4	5	5	3	3	4	4	4	4	5	3	5	4	4	6	4	4	76
USA	Round 2	4	4	4	4	4	5	5	3	4	4	5	4	4	5	4	4	4	4	75-151
John Cook	Round 1	4	4	5	5	3	5	4	3	4	5	4	4	5	3	5	5	3	5	76
USA	Round 2	4	4	4	4	4	4	4	4	3	5	7	4	4	3	4	4	4	5	75-151
Bob Tway	Round 1	4	4	4	5	3	5	4	5	4	5	5	5	4	3	5	5	3	5	78
USA	Round 2	5	3	4	5	3	5	4	3	3	5	5	3	4	3	4	5	4	5	73-151
Vanslow Phillips	Round 1	5	4	4	4	3	4	4	3	5	5	8	4	4	4	6	5	3	5	80
England	Round 2	4	4	4	5	3	5	4	3	4	4	4	4	3	4	4	5	3	4	71-151
Thomas Gogele	Round 1	5	4	4	4	3	5	4	3	4	4	4	5	5	4	4	6	3	5	76
Germany	Round 2	3	3	4	6	4	5	4	5	4	4	6	3	5	3	4	4	5	3	75-151
Warren Bladon	Round 1	4	5	4	4	3	5	4	3	5	6	5	4	5	3	5	5	4	4	78
England	Round 2	4	4	4	5	3	5	4	3	4	5	4	5	4	3	5	5	3	5	74-152
Miguel Angel Jimenez	Round 1	4	4	4	4	3	4	4	5	4	5	7	5	6	5	4	6	3	5	82
Spain	Round 2	4	4	4	3	3	4	4	3	4	4	5	3	4	4	4	5	3	5	70-152

HOLE		1	2	3	4	5	6	7	8	9	10	11	12	13	14	15	16	17	18	
PAR		4	4	4	5	3	5	4	3	4	4	4	4	4	3	4	5	3	4	TOTAL
Kim Jong Duck	Round 1	3	4	4	4	3	5	4	3	4	4	5	5	7	3	5	5	5	4	77
Korea	Round 2	4	5	3	5	3	4	4	3	5	4	4	6	4	3	4	5	4	5	75-152
Larry Batchelor	Round 1	3	4	4	4	4	5	4	5	4	5	6	4	5	3	4	5	3	5	77
England	Round 2	4	4	4	4	3	5	3	3	4	5	7	4	4	3	4	5	4	5	75-152
Cameron Clark	Round 1	4	4	5	5	3	5	4	4	4	4	4	4	4	4	5	6	4	6	79
England	Round 2	4	3	4	4	3	5	5	3	4	3	5	5	4	3	4	5	4	5	73-152
Sam Torrance	Round 1	5	5	4	4	4	5	5	3	5	4	5	4	5	3	4	5	3	5	78
Scotland	Round 2	4	5	3	5	4	4	5	3	4	5	4	4	4	3	5	4	3	5	74-152
Russell Claydon	Round 1	4	4	4	5	4	5	4	3	5	5	4	6	4	2	4	5	6	5	79
England	Round 2	4	4	4	5	3	5	4	3	5	4	4	4	3	3	4	5	3	6	73-152
Andrew Crerar	Round 1	3	4	4	4	3	5	4	4	4	5	5	5	5	3	6	5	3	4	76
Scotland	Round 2	4	4	4	5	3	6	4	3	5	5	5	5	4	3	5	4	3	5	77-153
*Daniel Olsson	Round 1	5	4	4	4	3	5	5	3	5	6	6	6	4	3	4	5	3	5	80
Sweden	Round 2	4	4	4	4	1	6	4	2	4	4	6	5	5	4	3	5	4	4	73-153
Mike Bradley	Round 1	3	4	4	4	3	4	4	3	5	5	6	5	5	3	4	6	4	5	77
USA	Round 2	4	4	3	4	3	6	4	2	4	6	5	5	4	4	5	5	3	5	76-153
Grant Dodd	Round 1	4	4	5	4	3	5	4	4	3	4	5	4	4	4	5	5	5	6	78
Australia	Round 2	3	4	4	4	3	5	4	3	4	6	7	4	4	2	4	5	4	5	75-153
*Shaun Webster	Round 1	4	4	5	5	3	4	4	3	4	6	4	4	5	2	5	6	3	4	75
England	Round 2	4	4	4	5	4	6	4	4	4	3	5	4	5	3	5	5	4	5	78-153
Sandy Lyle	Round 1	4	4	4	5	3	6	4	4	4	5	5	4	5	4	5	5	3	4	78
Scotland	Round 2	4	4	4	6	3	6	4	3	4	4	5	5	5	2	5	5	2	4	75-153
Jean Van de Velde	Round 1	4	4	4	4	3	5	4	4	4	6	4	5	4	3	4	5	4	6	77
France	Round 2	4	4	4	4	3	4	4	4	4	5	5	5	4	3	5	6	4	4	76-153
Per Haugsrud	Round 1	4	4	5	4	3	4	3	5	5	5	5	5	5	4	5	5	4	4	79
Norway	Round 2	4	4	5	5	4	5	4	3	4	4	4	4	5	3	4	5	4	4	75-154
Mike Miller	Round 1	4	4	4	5	4	5	4	3	5	7	6	5	5	3	5	4	4	5	82
Scotland	Round 2	4	4	4	5	3	4	4	3	4	5	4	4	4	3	5	4	3	5	72-154
Hirofumi Miyase	Round 1	4	4	5	5	3	4	5	4	5	5	4	5	4	3	4	6	3	6	79
Japan	Round 2	4	4	5	5	3	5	5	3	4	4	5	4	4	2	5	4	5	4	75-154
Ross McFarlane	Round 1	4	4	4	4	3	4	4	5	4	5	5	5	7	3	4	6	4	5	80
England	Round 2	4	5	4	4	3	5	4	4	5	4	4	4	4	2	5	6	3	4	74-154
Jeff Remesy	Round 1	4	4	4	4	3	5	4	4	4	4	5	5	5	4	5	6	4	5	79
France	Round 2	4	4	3	6	3	4	3	4	4	6	5	4	4	3	6	5	3	4	75-154
Dudley Hart	Round 1	4	4	3	4	4	5	4	3	4	4	4	5	5	3	6	6	4	6	78
USA	Round 2	3	4	4	5	3	4	6	3	4	4	6	4	4	3	6	6	4	4	77-155
Richard Green	Round 1	4	4	4	4	3	4	6	3	4	5	7	4	7	4	4	6	4	3	80
Australia	Round 2	5	4	5	4	3	5	5	3	4	4	5	5	3	3	4	5	4	4	75-155
Klas Eriksson	Round 1	3	4	5	4	3	5	4	4	4	6	7	5	5	5	5	6	3	7	85
Sweden	Round 2	4	4	4	4	3	4	5	3	3	5	4	4	4	3	4	4	4	4	70-155
Mark Roe	Round 1	4	4	5	4	3	4	3	3	4	5	9	4	4	3	7	4	4	5	79
England	Round 2	4	5	4	4	3	4	4	3	5	5	6	4	4	3	4	5	3	5	76-155
Andrew Sandywell	Round 1	4	4	3	5	4	6	4	3	4	5	6	6	5	3	4	5	4	5	80
England	Round 2	4	4	4	5	3	4	4	4	4	5	5	5	4	3	4	5	4	4	75-155
Phil Hinton	Round 1	4	4	4	4	2	5	4	3	4	5	5	5	5	4	6	7	2	5	78
England	Round 2	4	4	4	5	3	4	5	4	5	5	5	3	5	4	5	5	3	4	77-155
Gary Murphy	Round 1	4	4	4	6	3	5	4	3	4	5	8	4	4	4	5	5	4	8	84
Ireland	Round 2	4	4	4	5	4	5	4	3	4	3	4	5	4	3	4	5	3	4	72-156

HOLE		1	2	3	4	5	6	7	8	9	10	11	12	13	14	15	16	17	18	
PAR		4	4	4	5	3	5	4	3	4	4	4	4	4	3	4	5	3	4	TOTAL
Paul Stankowski	Round 1	4	4	5	4	3	6	5	2	5	4	5	4	7	3	4	5	5	5	80
USA	Round 2	4	4	5	5	3	4	4	3	4	5	7	4	6	3	3	5	3	4	76-156
Shigenori Mori	Round 1	4	4	5	4	3	5	5	3	4	5	5	4	5	4	5	5	5	5	80
Japan	Round 2	4	4	4	4	4	7	4	3	5	6	4	3	4	3	4	5	4	4	76-156
Ken Duke	Round 1	4	5	4	5	3	5	4	2	4	5	7	4	5	3	5	6	4	5	80
USA	Round 2	4	4	4	4	4	5	4	4	4	5	5	4	4	3	5	5	3	5	76-156
Paul Azinger	Round 1	4	4	4	4	3	5	3	3	6	5	5	4	5	3	6	5	4	6	79
USA	Round 2	5	4	4	5	4	6	4	2	4	6	4	5	4	3	5	5	3	5	78-157
*Yetsyn Taylor	Round 1	5	4	4	4	5	5	4	3	5	6	5	4	4	3	6	6	4	4	81
Wales	Round 2	4	4	3	6	3	5	4	4	3	4	9	4	5	3	4	4	3	4	76-157
David Frost	Round 1	5	4	4	4	4	6	4	4	3	6	5	4	4	4	4	5	4	7	81
South Africa	Round 2	5	5	3	5	3	5	3	3	4	6	4	4	5	5	4	5	4	4	77-158
Mardan Mamat	Round 1	4	4	5	5	4	5	4	4	3	5	6	4	6	3	5	6	4	6	83
Singapore	Round 2	4	4	4	5	3	5	4	4	4	5	4	5	3	3	5	5	3	5	75-158
Brendan McGovern	Round 1	5	5	4	6	3	5	5	4	6	5	5	4	6	3	5	5	4	4	84
Ireland	Round 2	5	4	4	5	3	4	4	3	4	4	5	4	4	3	4	5	4	5	74-158
*Steven Young	Round 1	5	4	4	6	3	4	4	3	4	4	5	5	5	3	5	6	3	6	79
Scotland	Round 2	4	4	4	5	3	5	4	3	5	4	6	4	4	3	5	7	5	5	80-159
Raphael Jacquelin	Round 1	4	4	5	5	3	4	4	4	4	6	5	5	6	4	5	5	3	5	81
France	Round 2	6	3	4	5	4	5	5	3	4	5	5	4	5	3	5	5	3	4	78-159
Steven Bottomley	Round 1	3	3	4	5	3	5	4	7	4	5	6	3	7	3	5	4	4	4	79
England	Round 2	5	4	5	4	3	4	4	10	4	4	5	4	4	4	4	5	3	5	81-160
Alexander Cejka	Round 1	3	5	5	5	6	4	5	3	3	4	6	4	5	3	5	5	3	7	81
Germany	Round 2	4	5	4	5	4	6	4	3	4	7	4	5	4	3	5	5	4	4	80-161
Gaurav Ghei	Round 1	4	4	5	4	3	5	4	4	4	5	6	4	4	4	5	6	3	7	81
India	Round 2	4	4	4	5	3	5	5	3	5	5	4	5	5	3	5	7	4	5	81-162
Nobuhito Sato	Round 1	4	6	4	5	3	6	4	3	4	7	5	5	5	4	5	7	4	4	85
Japan	Round 2	4	4	4	5	4	5	4	4	4	4	4	6	5	4	5	5	3	4	78-163
Dennis Edlund	Round 1	4	5	4	5	4	6	4	3	5	7	5	5	6	4	7	5	4	4	87
Sweden	Round 2	4	4	4	5	3	6	5	1	4	5	5	4	3	4	5	5	6	4	77-164
*James Miller	Round 1	5	4	4	4	4	4	4	3	5	6	4	4	5	3	6	5	4	6	80
England	Round 2	4	4	4	4	3	6	4	2	6	5	7	5	5	7	4	6	2	6	84-164
Naomichi (Joe) Ozaki	Round 1	4	4	5	5	4	6	4	2	4	4	4	5	5	3	4	5	2	6	76-WD
Japan																				
Chris Perry	Round 1	4	4	5	4	3	4	5	3	4	4	6	4	6	3	5	6	5	5	80-WD
USA																				
Yoshinori Kaneko	Round 1	4	5	4	5	4	5	5	5	5	5	7	4	4	3	4	5	4	6	84-WD
Japan																				
Ian Baker-Finch	Round 1	4	6	5	6	3	7	4	5	4	5	5	5	6	3	6	8	5	5	92-WD
Australia																				

CARD OF THE CHAMPIONSHIP COURSE

Hole	Yards	Par	Hole	Yards	Par
1	364	4	10	438	4
2	391	4	11	463	4
3	379	4	12	431	4
4	557	5	13	465	4
5	210	3	14	179	3
6	577	5	15	457	4
7	402	4	16	542	5
8	126	3	17	223	3
9	423	4	18	452	4
Out	3429	36	In	3650	35
			Out	3429	36
			Total	7079	71

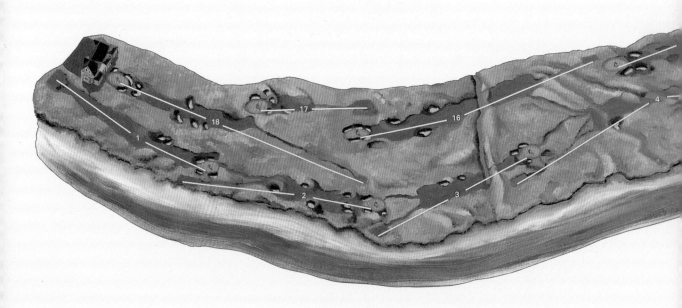